As Easy As 123

A Mostly-Macrobiotic Cookbook

Pamela Henkel and Lee Koch

Edited by Laurel Ruggles

George Ohsawa Macrobiotic Foundation
Oroville, California

Macrobiotic Cookbooks from the George Ohsawa Macrobiotic
Foundation include
  Basic Macrobiotic Cooking by Julia Ferre
  The Calendar Cookbook by Cornellia Aihara
  Cooking with Rachel by Rachel Albert
  The Do of Cooking by Cornellia Aihara
  The First Macrobiotic Cookbook by G.O.M.F.
A complete catalog of macrobiotic books is available from the
Foundation at the address below.

First Edition   1990

© copyright 1990 by Pamela Henkel and Lee Koch
Published by the George Ohsawa Macrobiotic Foundation
1511 Robinson Street, Oroville, California 95965
(916) 533-7702

Library of Congress number: 90-82651
ISBN 0-918860-51-2

Foreword

I am very happy to introduce this new cookbook by Pamela Henkel and Lee Koch. I first met Pam several years ago when she participated in one of our Vega Study Center intensives and later at the French Meadows Summer Camp which she attended with her husband Lee and their son. She has had much experience teaching macrobiotics and giving cooking classes in their Macro-Dome Natural Foods Cooking Center in Wisconsin.

Mostly, I have enjoyed reading this book because it contains many creative recipes; for example, soy milk is used in Western-style dishes and spices are used to balance the flavor of miso. It is especially helpful for those new to macrobiotic cooking and for those who desire recipes with a not-so-strict approach.

As Easy As 1, 2, 3 is a very practical book and includes short-time, quick and easy recipes and well-balanced cooking. Pam and Lee now have two children and they have learned to create many good snacks for them. Everyone will enjoy these ideas as well as the cooking-while-traveling section.

I recommend this book and hope that the many ideas included here will inspire you to create and improve your own cooking style.

Cornellia Aihara
Oroville, California

Preface

My purpose in writing this cookbook was to achieve balance; my own inner balance. I wanted to share with others a process of transition to a healthier eating pattern as I experienced it.

While living at the Vega Study Center in Oroville, California, many new insights came to me: For the first time I actually realized that what I did or did not put in my mouth makes a profound difference to the rest of the world. I realized that over-eating was actually taking away from the many mouths all over the world who cannot get enough to eat.

I also realized that eating many of the animal foods I was raised on was counter-productive to my own personal health as well as to my concern for the rest of the world's food supply.

This collection of recipes reflects my new attitudes about eating. It is my hope that you too may experience peace and pleasure as you share your meals and know that your actions make a difference.

Pamela Henkel
Wausau, Wisconsin

Introduction
Mostly Macrobiotic

In order to be "mostly macrobiotic," one must first have
an idea of what macrobiotics is. Herman Aihara, macrobiotic teacher, writer, and lecturer, has defined macrobiotics in this way:

"Macrobiotics amounts to finding our physiological
limitations and trying to live within them. This is the
cultivation of humbleness. When we think we can do
anything we want, we become arrogant. This arrogance
causes sickness.

When we are living within our physical limitations,
then our spirituality is free. Macrobiotics seeks freedom
in spirit. Freedom exists in our spirit – so we can think
anything. But biologically, physiologically we are unfree. We can wish to eat anything we want. But we cannot do it.

Disciplining physical unfreedom is the foundation of
spiritual freedom. God didn't give us unlimited biologi-
cal freedom, but appreciating and taking into considera-
tion our unfree physical condition leads us to greater
freedom, both physically and spiritually."

So – what reason do I have for writing a mostly-
macrobiotic cookbook? It is to help myself and others
maintain a balanced perspective on eating as it relates
to spiritual values.

Macrobiotics has helped me become creative, more
sensitive, more loving towards myself and others. However, this has happened with what I call an 85-percent

3

attitude. By 85-percent attitude I mean that I continually let go of perfection, and accept progress; I accept myself as I am and at the same time recognize my inner desire to become. With this attitude, anything I eat already is macrobiotic! The food becomes less important as my awareness of each and every moment of life increases in importance. It is with this attitude that I can continually learn how to better feed myself both physically and spiritually.

These recipes have been written with the busy families of our time in mind. Our attempt has been to apply the simple, whole-food choices of macrobiotics to some very quick, easy, and practical recipes. Learning some new terms and purchasing a few new supplies is not so very difficult if we can resist the desire to be perfect or to change 100 percent.

Contents

How to Cook Mostly-Macrobiotic Meals in Less Time Than You Thought Possible

One of the biggest challenges of cooking with whole foods and living in a more natural way is finding enough time in our busy lives. The following ideas have helped us to prepare food quicker and left us with time to enjoy ourselves and learn new things.

Cooking Grains and Beans Ahead

One way to save time in meal preparation is to consistently cook grains and beans ahead of time. Just about any meal that we make does use a grain. Beans are remarkably versatile and a few of them provide an added touch to a variety of meals.

Cooking ahead allows us the flexibility to prepare food in the evening or the early morning or whenever we have a little extra time. This is especially helpful when we work during the day and helps reduce the amount of time needed to prepare an evening or lunch meal.

Storage of the cooked grains or beans is not difficult, and they don't usually last long anyway. As an example, if we cook a pot of rice in the morning, it is usually gone by the next day. Cooked beans and grains can be stored a few days in the refrigerator in covered glass or plastic containers. They may even be stored in a freezer until needed. It is a good idea to freeze beans and grains in serving-sized containers so all the food can be used when it has been thawed. Once food is thawed, we prefer using it as soon as possible.

Below are some examples of recipes where we use cooked rice:

Brown Rice Salad or Nutty Rice Salad
Fried Rice or Rice Tempeh Rolls
Brown Rice Pizza Crust
Rice Muffins or Rice Bread
Stuffed Nori, rice balls, or nori rolls
add rice to oatmeal cereal or pancakes

Here are some possible uses of cooked beans:

Bean Sandwich Spread
Assorted Beans and Grains
Noodle Bean Squash Casserole
Garbanzo Tostada
nachos

One thing that has helped us to be open to all the possible uses for grains and beans is to cook ahead and then decide on a recipe or make up a new one. It is a great way to try new recipes or make our own. We have had some wonderful meals and some that we have chosen to forget. The first thing to develop is a good basic method for cooking grains and beans.

Basic Grain Recipes

A well-cooked grain is a great delight, requires some time, energy, and practice, but is worth the effort. We recommend a pressure cooker for rice, but a pan or pot will do.

P ressure-cooked rice

2 cups short-grain brown rice
3 to 3¼ cups water
small amount of sea salt or 6-inch strip of kombu

1 Wash rice by stirring it in a bowl with water and then draining it in a strainer.

2 Place rice, water, and salt or kombu in the pressure cooker.

3 Cook the rice over medium or high heat until the pressure valve starts to jiggle.

4 Turn heat to low and use a flame spreader to keep the rice from burning.

5 Cook for about 40 minutes and then turn off heat and let the rice sit until the pressure is down.

We experimented to determine how we liked our rice. Adding more or less water can give a different flavor and texture to the rice.

Use some "added attractions" for a new flavor and texture. Some possibilities are: rye and wheat berries, sweet brown rice, wild rice, barley, lentils. Presoaking these additions is helpful as they take a little longer to cook. Soak about ¼ cup of the extra grain in ½ cup of water for a few hours.

Boiled rice

    1 cup brown rice
    2 cups water or vegetable stock
    pinch of sea salt

1 Wash and drain the rice.

2 Put the rice, water, and salt in a pot.

3 Bring to a boil.

4 Cover tightly and simmer for 50 to 60 minutes with no stirring.

Parboiled rice

    1 cup brown rice
    1½ cups water

1 Bring rice to boil, and then simmer for about 20 minutes.

2 Spread the rice on a cookie sheet and bake at 200°F for 1 hour, stirring often.

3 When cool, package in airtight container. Refrigeration is not necessary.

4 To complete the cooking, boil the rice with approximately 2 cups water for 15 to 20 minutes depending on desired consistency.

This method is ideal for traveling.

Sweet brown rice

2 cups sweet brown rice
3¼ cups water

1 Wash and drain rice.

2 Place rice and water in a pressure cooker.

3 Bring to pressure over high heat.

4 Reduce heat to low and cook for 45 to 55 minutes, using a flame spreader.

Boiled millet

1 cup millet
3 cups water
pinch of sea salt

1 Wash the millet and then drain.

2 For better flavor dry roast the millet in a skillet over medium heat.

3 Add the water and salt and bring to a boil.

4 Cover and simmer for 20 to 25 minutes.

We prefer pan-boiled millet to millet cooked in a pressure cooker.

Pressure-cooked millet

> 2 cups millet
> 5 cups water
> pinch of sea salt or a small piece of kombu

1 Wash and drain millet.

2 Place millet, water, and salt or kombu in a pressure cooker.

3 Cook over high heat until the pressure valve starts to jiggle.

4 Turn heat to low and cook for 20 to 25 minutes, using a flame spreader.

Roasted millet

> 1 cup millet

1 Wash millet in a bowl and then drain.

2 Roast the millet in a dry skillet over high heat, stirring constantly, until millet becomes golden and crunchy. Or, spread the millet on a cookie sheet and place in the oven at 300°F for about 30 minutes.

3 Store in an airtight container.

P arboiled millet

> 1 cup millet
> 2 cups water

1 Bring millet to a boil, then simmer about 15 minutes.

2 Spread on a cookie sheet and bake at 200°F for 1 hour, stirring often.

3 When cool, package in airtight container. Refrigeration is not necessary.

4 To complete the cooking, boil millet for 5 to 7 minutes in 2 cups water.

This method is ideal for traveling.

Basic Bean Recipes

L entils

> 1 cup lentils
> 1½ to 2 cups water

1 Wash the lentils and put in a pan with water.

2 Bring to a boil. Cover and simmer for 45 minutes.

3 Add extra water if necessary.

A zuki beans

1 cup azuki beans
4 cups water
6-inch strip kombu

1 Wash beans and place in a pot with kombu and half of the water.

2 Bring to a boil and simmer, covered, for about 30 minutes.

3 Add rest of water and then simmer for 1 hour or until the beans are tender.

G arbanzo beans

1 cup garbanzo beans
3 cups water
6-inch strip kombu

1 Wash beans and soak overnight. Drain beans.

2 Place beans, kombu, and 3 cups of fresh water in a pressure cooker.

3 Bring to pressure over high heat.

4 Reduce heat and simmer 45 minutes.

P into beans

> 1 cup pinto beans
> 3 cups water
> 6-inch strip kombu

1 Soak beans in water overnight. Drain beans.

2 Place beans, 3 cups of fresh water, and kombu in a pressure cooker.

3 Bring to pressure over high heat.

4 Reduce heat and simmer for 15 minutes.

P re-cooked tofu

> 1 lb. tofu
> ¼ cup sesame oil

1 Heat oil in pan and crumble tofu into hot oil.

2 Fry until brown, stirring constantly, about 5 minutes.

3 Drain off excess oil and cool tofu.

4 Place in airtight container.

This method is ideal for travel. Pre-cooked tofu will keep for 4 to 5 days without refrigeration.

Time-Saving Strategies

Simple Seasonings
Seasonings such as gomashio, tekka, shoyu, dehydrated vegetables, shoyu-roasted squash seeds, soy mayonnaise, and miso mustard can help turn cooked grains and beans or simple leftovers into a delicious meal. For example, cooked brown rice or leftover noodles become gourmet rice or noodles when combined with dehydrated vegetables, roasted squash seeds, dried miso soup, shoyu, a touch of water to mix, and then heated or baked until warm.

Flexibility
Substitution of recipe ingredients helps to save time and create an endless variety of new dishes. It reduces the need to run to the store to get a certain vegetable or spend time cooking rice when you have some millet. For example, in the Broccoli with Miso Onion Sauce recipe, cauliflower can be substituted for the broccoli. By altering the vegetable or grain in any recipe a new distinctive flavor is created.

Use of Efficient Processed Foods
Some packaged/processed foods we have found useful in an effort to save time or while traveling or camping are:

> rizcous
> couscous
> falafel
> burger mixes
> rice cakes
> corn tostada and taco shells

ramen noodles
whole-wheat pita bread
quick-cooking rice
rolled oats
brown-rice, millet, and amaranth cereals
dried soups
rice pilaf and other ethnic mixes
amasake
soy cheese
vegetable seasoning
soy mayonnaise
dehydrated vegetables
egg roll wrappers

Important considerations in the purchase or use of processed products are:

• Check ingredients for salt, sweeteners, and other additives. It is possible to buy natural varieties of all these products.

• When we travel we buy these products before leaving on a trip as they are often hard to find quickly.

• We try not to allow these to become our regular fare, but use them wisely when we need them.

Crunchy Toppings

A crunchy topping makes any dish a delight and can quickly add zip to leftovers. Some of our favorites are:

Main Dishes: soy nuts, sunflower seeds, sesame seeds, roasted millet.

Desserts: roasted rolled oats or millet, unsweetened carob chips, puffed brown rice or millet cereals, raisins and other dried fruit.

Mochi

Mochi is a delicious and nutritious food made from

sweet brown rice. It is very versatile and can be used as a snack or meal by itself; or stuffed with cooked squash, tofu sauce, nut butters, applesauce, refried beans or hummus, sautéed vegies, soy cheese, fruit or fruit sauce; or grated as a topping for main dishes or desserts.

One-Pot Meals
One-pot meals save time in both the preparation and cleanup. In addition it is possible to achieve balance with the use of grains, beans, vegetables, and sea vegetables. A one-pot meal is great for traveling or camping, especially since we have a single-burner stove.

A one-pot meal can be prepared in stages over a period of time and then assembled just before eating. Another approach is to assemble the dish ahead and cook at a later time. This is very helpful for working people as it allows us to make a dish in the morning and just put it into the oven when we get home.

What To Do with the Time You Save
A real joy of eating as we have outlined is the extra energy that we have. We have often used this energy to cook more or work harder in some other area of our lives. Slowly we are beginning to use this time and energy to explore new ways of accepting and enjoying ourselves.

If we just use these tips to work harder and not enjoy life more, then we have missed something on our journey.

Main Dishes
Vegetable Dishes

O

riental coleslaw

> 1 large carrot, shredded
> 2 cups Chinese cabbage, shredded
> 1 to 2 cups bean sprouts
> 1 Tbsp. kelp powder
> ¼ tsp. cayenne or chili powder
> 3 tsp. sesame oil
> 2 tsp. shoyu
> ½ cup chopped parsley
> 2 sheets nori

1 Toss carrots, cabbage, and bean sprouts.

2 Add kelp and cayenne or chili powder, mixing thoroughly.

3 Press in a salad press or place in a bowl, set a plate on top of the vegetables and weight the plate with a jar of water or a clean rock.

4 Refrigerate overnight.

5 Drain liquid and toss vegetables with oil, shoyu, and parsley.

6 Crisp nori in oven for about 30 seconds at 300°F or over a burner until nori becomes green. Shred nori and sprinkle over vegetables.

4 servings   overnight

Broccoli with miso onion sauce

2 cups broccoli, cut into small flowerettes
1 package of natural onion soup mix (dry)
water
1 tsp. brown-rice miso
2 Tbsp. Tofu Mayonnaise or other soy mayonnaise
¼ cup plain soy milk
2 scallions, chopped

1 Steam broccoli until it is done to desired tenderness.

2 While broccoli is steaming, add water to natural onion soup mix, usually about ⅔ of indicated amount to achieve thicker mixture.

3 Add miso, soy mayonnaise, and soy milk to soup mix, and mix well to make a sauce.

4 Heat the sauce and pour over broccoli.

5 Top with scallions.

🍴 4 servings   ⏲ 10–15 minutes

Cucumber wakame salad

1 cucumber, sliced
2 medium carrots, sliced
1 tsp. sea salt
½ cup wakame, soaked 4 minutes and sliced into
    small pieces
4 Tbsp. apple juice

1 Mix cucumber, carrots, and salt and let set overnight. Use a salad press if you have one.

2 Pour off liquid from the cucumber-carrot mixture and drain in a colander or sieve.

3 Place cucumber, carrots, and wakame in serving bowl and pour apple juice over the top.

🍴 3–4 servings   📅 overnight

Simple, elegant Swiss chard

> 3 cups Swiss chard, chopped
> 1 medium onion, chopped
> ½ cup parsley, chopped
> 1 Tbsp. oil
> ½ tsp. cayenne
> ½ tsp. kelp powder
> ¼ tsp. nutmeg
> ¼ tsp. coriander
> ¼ cup water
> ½ cup dulse, arame, or wakame, soaked and chopped
> ¾ cup cooked rice

1 Combine the first nine ingredients and simmer for 10 to 12 minutes.

2 Stir in the sea vegetable and rice and simmer for another 10 minutes.

🍴 4–6 servings   📅 30 minutes

V egetable pancakes

2 tsp. kuzu
½ cup bok choy, finely chopped
½ cup carrots, finely shredded
¼ cup onion, finely chopped
¼ cup green pepper, finely chopped
½ cup brown-rice flour
1 tsp. shoyu
3 Tbsp. water

1 Stir together all ingredients adjusting the amount of water to achieve desired consistency.

2 Spoon ¼ cup mixture onto hot oiled griddle and cook approximately 3 minutes each side.

3–4 servings   20 minutes

H ijiki salad

½ cup hijiki
water to cover hijiki
1 Tbsp. shoyu
1 tsp. sea salt
2 cups corn (about 4 ears)
½ cup peas
½ cup cucumber, sliced
½ cup carrot, grated
Sesame dressing:
1 Tbsp. prepared miso mustard
2 Tbsp. sesame butter
2 Tbsp. brown rice vinegar
3 Tbsp. boiling water

1 Wash and soak hijiki, then slice into ½-inch lengths.

2 Place hijiki and soaking water in pot. Bring to a boil, cover and reduce heat to simmer for 20 minutes.

3 Add shoyu and cook for 20 minutes until water is evaporated.

4 Meanwhile, bring another pot of water to boil with 1 teaspoon salt and cook corn until tender.

5 Remove corn from the cooking water and when cool, cut kernels from the cobs.

6 Bring peas to a boil in same water for 3 to 4 minutes and let cool.

7 In bowl mix hijiki, peas, cucumber, grated carrot, and corn.

8 Blend dressing ingredients together until smooth and mix into salad.

🍴 4 servings   ▣ 45 minutes

Vegetable and Tofu Dishes

C orn salad

1 block tofu
3 ears corn on the cob
1½ cups snow peas
1 onion, chopped
1 tsp. sesame oil
1 tsp. rice vinegar or umeboshi vinegar
1 sheet nori, torn into narrow strips

1 Blanch tofu about 20 minutes in salted water. Cube or crumble tofu.

2 Boil corn in salted water. Cut and scrape kernels off cob.

3 Blanch snow peas about 20 seconds in salted water.

4 Toss all ingredients together in bowl with oil and vinegar. Garnish with nori strips.

🍴 3–4 servings   📷 25 minutes

Spinach fried tofu

> 1 Tbsp. shoyu
> 1½ tsp. dark sesame oil
> 1 tsp. rice syrup
> ¼ tsp. kelp powder
> ¼ tsp. cayenne
> ½ lb. tofu, pressed between two plates and drained
> oil for frying tofu
> 3 to 4 cups water
> 1 lb. spinach, washed
> 2 sheets nori, cut into thin strips

1 Blend first five ingredients for a dressing and set aside.

2 Heat oil in wok or skillet and fry tofu on both sides.

3 Drain tofu on paper towel until cool and cut into thin strips.

4 Bring water to boil, drop in spinach and reduce heat to medium. Remove spinach in 20 seconds and pat dry.

Cut spinach into narrow strips.

5 Toss spinach with dressing and tofu, and top with nori.

🍴 4–6 servings   📺 20 minutes

Tofu au gratin

> 1 large onion, thinly sliced
> 2 to 3 Tbsp. oil or water
> ½ cup broccoli, chopped
> 2 cups tofu, cut in ¼-inch cubes
> 3 Tbsp. whole-wheat or brown-rice flour
> 1 small carton soy milk, 6 to 8 oz.
> 1 tsp. mustard (miso mustard is excellent)
> 1¼ cups soy cheese, grated
> 2 Tbsp. whole-grain bread crumbs

1 Preheat oven to 350°F.

2 Sauté onion in ½ to 1 tablespoon oil or water.

3 Add chopped broccoli and sauté 2 minutes more. Remove vegetables from skillet.

4 In same skillet, sauté tofu about 5 minutes, adding a little more oil or water to prevent sticking.

5 Heat 1 tablespoon oil in saucepan and add flour. Cook lightly for a few minutes stirring constantly until smooth and bubbly. Slowly stir in milk and cook over low heat until thick.

6 Remove from heat and stir in mustard and ¾ cup of the cheese.

7 Oil shallow oven-proof casserole dish. Layer with half the tofu, cover with half the sauce, then half the vegetables. Repeat the layers starting with the tofu. Top with bread crumbs and remaining cheese. Bake 20 minutes or until bubbly and brown on top.

🍴 4–6 servings   🖳 45 minutes

V egie casserole

> 8 oz. tofu or tempeh cut into small cubes; or cooked beans (any type)
> 1 onion, cut in ¼-inch crescents
> ½ carrot, cut in ¼-inch slices
> ½ parsnip, quartered and sliced
> ¼ head green cabbage, chopped
> ½ cup peas
> ½ tsp. thyme

Stock:
> 1 quart water or vegetable stock
> 1 Tbsp. shoyu
> 1 tsp. thyme

Gravy:
> 1 cup hot stock
> ⅓ to ½ cup brown-rice flour
> 2 Tbsp. shoyu

1 Pre-heat oven to 350°F.

2 Combine stock ingredients and bring to a boil. Cook tofu or tempeh in stock and remove.

3 Add root vegetables to stock. Bring to a boil, turn heat down and cook five minutes.

4 Drain vegies and make gravy from the stock.

5 To make gravy: Return 1 cup stock to pot, add flour and shoyu. Stir with wire whisk over medium-high heat until mixture becomes smooth and thick (1 to 2 minutes). Combine gravy with all vegetables. Add tempeh, tofu, or beans and mix well.

6 Transfer to oiled casserole, sprinkle ½ teaspoon thyme over top and bake until gravy bubbles, about 20 to 30 minutes.

🍴 6–8 servings   ▦ 60 minutes

H ijiki and dried tofu

4 or 5 dried shiitake mushrooms
1¼ cups dried hijiki (or arame)
1½ tsp. sesame oil
4 pieces dried tofu
¼ cup peas
1 carrot, sliced thinly
1 Tbsp. shoyu
2 tsp. mirin (optional)
2 Tbsp. minced parsley

1 Soak the mushrooms in water to cover for 3 hours. Drain and reserve soaking water. Discard stems and thinly slice caps.

2 Wash and soak hijiki.

3 Heat oil in skillet, add shiitake and sauté.

4 Drain hijiki and reserve soaking water. Add hijiki to

27

shiitake and sauté briefly.

5 Add soaking water from hijiki and shiitake and additional fresh water to almost cover. Bring to boil, lower heat and simmer 10 minutes, covered.

6 Meanwhile soak dried tofu for 5 minutes, then squeeze out excess water. Dice tofu, add it to the pan and toss.

7 Place carrots and peas on top of hijiki mixture and add shoyu and mirin. Cover pot and cook for 10 minutes. Toss.

8 If liquid remains, cook uncovered over medium heat until nearly dry.

9 Sprinkle parsley over, cover, and steam for 1 minute.

🍴 3–4 servings   ▥ 25 minutes
(if mushrooms pre-soaked)

Grain and Vegetable Dishes

Baked cabbage bundles

½ cup walnuts, chopped
shoyu
12 large cabbage leaves
boiling water
1 cup onions, chopped
1 tsp. toasted sesame oil
1 cup cooked brown rice

1 Cover walnuts with light coating of shoyu and roast in oven at 300°F for about 8 minutes.

2 Cook cabbage leaves by dropping into boiling water for about 15 to 30 seconds.

3 Drain and pat cabbage leaves dry.

4 Sauté onions in sesame oil until golden. Combine rice, onions, and walnuts in bowl, adding a little shoyu to increase flavor if desired.

5 Roll this mixture into cabbage leaves and bake at 350°F for about 12 minutes.

🍴 8 servings   🖵 30–45 minutes

B rown rice salad

4 cups water
pinch of sea salt
½ cup carrots, chopped any style
¼ cup celery, diced
1½ cups cooked brown rice, cooled
½ cup wakame, soaked for 3 min. and sliced
½ cup parsley, chopped
¼ cup walnuts, roasted and chopped
½ cup cucumber, diced
Umeboshi mustard dressing:
3 Tbsp. miso mustard (or any type)
2 Tbsp. umeboshi vinegar
2 Tbsp. lemon juice

1 To boiling water, add pinch of sea salt.

2 Cook carrots 2 to 3 minutes and remove; then cook

celery 1 to 2 minutes and remove. Reserve cooking water to use in soup if desired.

3 Let vegetables cool and place in serving bowl.

4 Add cooked rice, wakame, parsley, chopped walnuts, and cucumber.

5 Combine dressing ingredients and toss salad with the dressing just before serving.

| 4 servings | 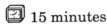 15 minutes |

Green pea rice

> 1 onion, chopped
> oil
> 1 cup cooked brown rice
> 2 tsp. shoyu
> 1½ cups cooked green peas or green pea soup
> ¼ lb. soysage (optional)

1 Sauté onion in small amount of oil.

2 Add brown rice and simmer 5 minutes.

3 Add shoyu to rice mixture and gradually add peas.

4 If using the soysage, add to rice and peas last. (You may want to brown the soysage in frying pan before adding to the rest.)

This tastes especially good served on a tostada shell.

| 3–4 servings |  15 minutes |

Sunnie burgers

½ cup sunflower seeds
¼ cup walnuts
½ cup onion, chopped
¾ cup carrots, shredded
2 tsp. shoyu
safflower or other oil, as needed
1 to 2 tsp. vegetable seasoning (powdered dehydrated vegetables) or other seasoning
1½ cups cooked brown rice
¼ to ½ cups brown-rice flour (or corn, wheat, or other flour)

1 Roast the sunflower seeds and the walnuts in oven at 350°F for about 10 minutes.

2 Sauté onion and carrot in shoyu and oil as needed to prevent burning.

3 Chop the walnuts.

4 Put the sunflower seeds in bowl, adding the sautéed vegetables, walnuts, and seasoning.

5 Mix all ingredients adding rice, flour, and a small amount of water, if necessary, to obtain burger consistency.

6 Shape into patties and bake on a cookie sheet at about 350°F for about 10 to 12 minutes.

These burgers are especially good with miso mustard and bok choy leaves or lettuce.

🍴 4–6 servings   🍽 25 minutes

F ried rice

roasted sesame oil
1½ cups onions, diced
¾ cup carrots, matchsticks
3 sheets nori torn into strips and soaked 3 to 4 minutes (reserve soaking water)
½ cup celery, diced
2 Tbsp. shoyu
2 cups cooked brown rice
2 Tbsp. ginger juice, squeezed from grated ginger
½ cup almonds, roasted and chopped

1 Lightly oil pan and sauté onions 5 to 7 minutes.

2 Add carrots and nori and cook 5 to 7 minutes.

3 Add celery and 2 tablespoons shoyu and cook 5 minutes.

4 Add cooked brown rice, 3 to 4 tablespoons soaking
water from nori, 2 tablespoons ginger juice and mix together. Simmer until heated through.

5 Add chopped roasted almonds.

6–8 servings   30 minutes

S tuffed nori

2 sheets nori
1 cup cooked brown rice, millet, barley, or kasha
½ cup carrots, grated
4 Tbsp. sesame seeds, roasted
1 Tbsp. lemon juice

1 Tbsp. prepared mustard
1 Tbsp. brown-rice vinegar

1 Toast nori 10 inches above flame or burner for 3 to 5 seconds.

2 Cut nori into quarters, roll each quarter sheet into cone shape, wet edges, and stick together.

3 Place remaining ingredients in bowl and mix together.

4 Fill cones with mixture and serve.

¶¶ 3–4 servings   ▣ 15 minutes

Dried vegetable egg rolls

1 cup dehydrated vegetables, any kind
1 tsp. mirin (optional)
1 tsp. brown-rice vinegar
1 tsp. sesame oil
1 cup cooked brown rice
1 package egg roll wrappers, whole wheat if possible
   (16 oz.)

1 Sauté dehydrated vegetables in mirin, brown-rice vinegar, and sesame oil.

2 Preheat oven to 350°F.

3 Combine vegetables with brown rice and wrap in egg roll wrappers.

4 Bake at 350°F for 10 to 12 minutes.

¶¶ 8 servings   ▣ 30–45 minutes

As Easy As 1, 2, 3

Nutty rice salad

¼ cup walnuts, chopped
½ tsp. shoyu
¼ cup cooked brown rice
¼ cup cooked wild rice or millet
½ cup onion, minced
¼ cup celery, chopped finely
½ cup bok choy, chopped finely
2 tsp. umeboshi vinegar
1 tsp. mirin (optional)
¼ cup Tofu Mayonnaise or other soy mayonnaise

1 Mix walnuts with ½ tsp. shoyu and roast in oven at 300°F for 10 minutes.

2 Mix brown rice and wild rice or millet.

3 Sauté onions, bok choy, and celery, adding umeboshi vinegar and mirin. You may also add a little water as necessary.

4 Combine sautéed vegetables with rice and roasted walnuts.

5 Add mayonnaise to taste.

🍴 4–6 servings   ▣ 20 minutes

Rice vegie pilaf

½ cup water or vegetable stock (may include sea vegetable soaking juice)
1 carrot, chopped finely

1 onion, chopped finely
2 Tbsp. wakame, soaked and chopped finely
2 cups cooked rice
½ tsp. miso

1 Bring water, carrot, onion, and wakame to a boil for 1 to 2 minutes.

2 Continue cooking over medium-low heat for 3 to 5 minutes.

3 Add cooked rice and cook for at least 10 minutes longer over low heat.

4 When ready to serve, add miso and stir.

🍴 3–4 servings 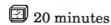 20 minutes

M illet salad

1 cup millet
kernels cut and scraped from 1 ear of corn
3 cups water
pinch sea salt
½ onion
1 carrot
1 tsp. rice vinegar
½ tsp. sea salt
¼ cup arame or wakame

1 Bring millet and corn to a boil in salted water and simmer for 20 minutes.

2 Slice onion, shred carrot, and mix with rice vinegar and sea salt. Let sit for 20 minutes.

3 Boil arame or wakame for 10 minutes. Drain and chop into small pieces.

4 Mix millet and corn with arame or wakame and vegetables.

5 Season to taste with more vinegar and shoyu if desired.

🍴 3–4 servings   📺 40 minutes

Millet egg rolls

1 cup millet
1 medium onion, minced
4 scallions, chopped
1½ cups bok choy, chopped
1 cup celery, chopped
1 to 2 tsp. sesame oil
1 to 2 tsp. shoyu
1 cup cooked brown rice
1 tsp. miso, any type
1 package egg roll wrappers, whole wheat if possible
    (16 oz.)

1 Roast millet on cookie sheet at 350°F for about 10 minutes.

2 Sauté onion, scallions, bok choy, and celery in sesame oil, adding shoyu as desired for flavor.

3 Combine millet, rice, and miso with sautéed vegetables in bowl.

4 Put about ⅓ cup of mixture on each egg roll wrapper and roll up.

5 Bake at 350°F for about 10 minutes.

🍴 8 servings   40 minutes

Arame oatmeal

> ¼ cup dry arame
> soaking water for arame
> 3 cups water or vegetable stock
> 1 cup diced vegetables (carrots, onions, broccoli, and
> cauliflower work well)
> 1 to 1⅓ cups rolled oats, depending on consistency
> desired
> 2 tsp. barley miso

1 Soak arame in water 5 to 10 minutes.

2 Boil vegetable stock or water, then add diced vegetables and cook for 1 to 2 minutes.

3 Add rolled oats and boil over high heat 1 to 2 minutes; lower to medium heat and cook 5 to 7 minutes.

4 Cut arame into small pieces. Save soaking water for future stock.

5 Add arame to oatmeal mixture and turn heat to low. Cook 10 minutes and remove from heat.

6 Add barley miso and mix thoroughly.

🍴 4–6 servings   30 minutes

Oatmeal with fall vegetables

3 cups water or vegetable stock
¼ tsp. sea salt
3 leaves of a dark green vegetable (collards, kale,
    Swiss chard, or beet greens) chopped finely
1 to 1⅓ cups rolled oats
1 cup cooked squash, any type, cut in chunks
3 Tbsp. soy milk (optional)
squash seeds, roasted (optional)

1 Boil water and add ¼ teaspoon salt.

2 Add greens and boil 1 minute.

3 Add rolled oats and cook over high heat 1 to 2 minutes, then over medium heat for 5 to 7 minutes.

4 Add squash and turn heat to low for 5 to 7 minutes.

5 If desired, add soy milk and sprinkle squash seeds on top.

🍴 4–6 servings   ▦ 15 minutes

Oat burgers

1 cup onion, diced
½ cup rolled oats
½ cup dulse, soaked and finely sliced (or arame, wakame, or hijiki)
⅓ cup whole-grain flour (any type)
pinch of sea salt
sesame oil for frying

1 Mix onion, rolled oats, dulse, flour, and sea salt with enough of the dulse soaking water to make stiff mix.

2 Shape into 2-inch burgers, adding more dulse water or flour to obtain desired consistency.

3 Heat enough oil in pan to fry and brown burgers on both sides.

4 Drain on paper towels before serving.

🍴 4–6 servings   📺 15 minutes

Squash pie

1 tsp. toasted sesame oil
1 large butternut squash, peeled, seeded, and cut
     into bite-sized chunks
pinch of sea salt
¼ tsp. ginger juice, squeezed from grated ginger
2 Tbsp. kuzu
2 Tbsp. water
½ recipe Brown Rice Pie Crust, fitted in pie pan
Topping (optional):
2 onions, chopped
1 tsp. sesame oil
3 Tbsp. white miso
3 Tbsp. mirin

1 Heat sesame oil in large skillet, add squash, pinch of sea salt and sauté briefly.

2 Add water to cover bottom of pan, lower heat, cover, and simmer until tender (about 20 minutes). Add more water occasionally if needed.

3 Meanwhile, prepare onion topping, if desired, for a sweeter pie: Sauté onions in oil for 20 minutes, add miso and mirin and sauté 1 minute.

4 Add ginger juice to squash and toss.

5 Mash or blend squash mixture until smooth. Filling should have consistency of mashed potatoes. If too dry, add a little water.

6 Dissolve kuzu in 2 tablespoons water and mix with squash.

7 Spread the mixture into pie crust.

8 Spread onion topping over squash, if desired.

9 Bake at 350°F for 20 minutes.

🍴 8–10 servings   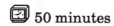 50 minutes

Mochi pie

2 cups vegetables, cut in medium diagonals (onions, broccoli, leeks, carrots work well)
1 Tbsp. kuzu dissolved in ¼ cup water
2 tsp. shoyu
1 tsp. ginger juice, squeezed from grated ginger
¼ to ½ cup soy cheese, shredded (optional)
1 tsp. miso, diluted in ¼ cup water
6 oz. mochi, shredded (mugwort or other)

1 Preheat oven to 350°F.

2 Sauté vegetables in very small amount of water.

3 Add shoyu and kuzu water to vegetables and mix to

thicken. Be sure to add kuzu while vegetables are hot.

4 Add ginger juice, diluted miso, and soy cheese.

5 Place mixture in pie pan and cover with shredded mochi.

6 Bake at 350° F for 20 to 30 minutes until mochi begins to brown on top.

🍴 4 servings   📺 50 minutes

Couscous egg rolls

1½ cups couscous
1¾ cups water
1 medium onion, chopped
1 cup bok choy, sliced
shoyu, to desired taste
1 cup green peas
1 Tbsp. miso, any type
¼ cup Tofu Mayonnaise, soy mayonnaise, or other
    salad dressing
8 to 10 egg roll wrappers, whole wheat if possible

1 Cook couscous in 1¾ cups water: Bring to a boil, then simmer for about 10 to 15 minutes.

2 Preheat oven to 350°F.

3 Sauté onion in small amount of water.

4 Add bok choy and about a teaspoon of shoyu. Turn burner off and add peas.

5 Combine the couscous with the miso, then add sautéed vegetables.

41

6 Use the soy mayonnaise or salad dressing as needed to make the mixture hold together.

7 Spread ¼ to ⅓ cup of the mixture on each egg roll wrapper and roll up. Bake at 350°F for about 10 minutes.

❚❚ 8 servings   ▢ 35 minutes

Sea vegie tostada

4 corn tostada shells
¼ cup arame
2 cups vegetables, chopped (onion, broccoli, carrot, and cucumber work well)
¼ cup vegetable stock or water
1 sheet nori
¼ cup Tofu Mayonnaise or other soy mayonnaise
1 Tbsp. prepared mustard
½ tsp. miso

1 Toast the corn tostada shells in oven at 300°F for about 5 to 8 minutes.

2 Soak arame in water for about 5 minutes, then drain.

3 Sauté vegetables in stock or water starting with onion.

4 Add rest of vegetables, one at a time, adding hardest ones first. Add arame.

5 Roast nori in oven for approximately 2 minutes at 200°F or over burner. Tear nori into strips.

6 Combine the cooked vegetables and the tofu mayonnaise in a bowl, adding the mustard and miso for flavor.

7 Heap the vegie mixture onto the tostada shells. Top with pieces of toasted nori and serve.

Try adding shredded soy cheese on top, and return to oven until cheese melts.

🍴 4 servings   📺 15 minutes

Seitan reuben

4 slices whole-grain bread
1 Tbsp. miso mustard
2 to 3 ozs. seitan
½ cup sauerkraut
4 slices onion
4 slices soy cheese (optional)
¼ cup Tofu Mayonnaise (optional)

1 Spread slices of bread with miso mustard.

2 Warm bread in oven for 3 to 4 minutes.

3 Slice seitan thinly.

4 Layer sauerkraut, seitan, onion, and cheese (if using) on each slice of bread.

5 Bake in oven at 350°F for 3 to 4 minutes.

6 Top with mayonnaise, if desired.

🍴 4 servings   📺 10 minutes

Vegetable and Noodle Dishes

S hiitake taco

1 medium onion, chopped
4 shiitake mushrooms, soaked and chopped
1 tsp. shoyu
2 tsp. miso mustard
2 to 4 taco shells
2 tsp. kuzu
2 tsp. water
½ cup whole-wheat noodles, cooked

1 Saute onion in small amount of water for about 3 minutes.

2 Add shiitake mushrooms and shoyu and saute 2 more minutes.

3 Spread miso mustard on taco shells and warm them in the oven for 3 to 4 minutes.

4 Dissolve kuzu in the 2 teaspoons water.

5 Add kuzu mixture to the onion-mushroom mixture and simmer, stirring, until mixture begins to thicken.

6 Line the taco shells with the cooked noodles.

7 Top noodles with the mushroom-onion sauce and warm in oven at 350°F for 3 to 4 minutes.

🍴 4 servings   ▣ 10 minutes

C abbage noodle tostada

4 to 6 oz. whole-grain noodles (mugwort or lotus root work well)
6 tostada shells (blue or yellow corn)
1 cup green cabbage, shredded
1 cup purple cabbage, shredded
4 oz. soy cheese, shredded (optional)
Miso Sauce:
  ½ cup Tofu Mayonnaise, soy mayonnaise, or creamy tofu
  1 tsp. miso, any type (barley, brown rice, dandelion, etc.)
  ½ tsp. umeboshi vinegar
  1 tsp. shoyu

1 Boil the noodles. Rinse and drain well.

2 Warm the tostada shells in the oven at 250°F for about 10 minutes.

3 Mix sauce ingredients until creamy. Add water if sauce is too thick.

4 Combine shredded green and purple cabbage with miso sauce.

5 Layer the noodles on top of the tostada shells, and top with cabbage mixture. Add shredded soy cheese, if you like, heating only until the cheese melts.

🍴 6 servings   ▣ 20 minutes

Sea noodle tostada

1 package wakame ramen noodles or other ramen
  noodles
4 tostada shells, (blue or yellow corn)
1 medium onion, chopped
1 medium leek, sliced thinly
2 to 3 oz. daikon, shredded (optional)
1 umeboshi plum, chopped
½ tsp. canola oil
2 tsp. water
1 cup cooked brown rice or millet
¼ cup sunflower seeds, roasted

1 Boil the wakame noodles until tender, about 10 minutes. Rinse and drain well.

2 Warm the tostada shells in oven at 350° F for about 3 minutes.

3 Sauté the onion, leek, daikon, and umeboshi plum in oil and water until soft and translucent.

4 Assemble as follows: Layer wakame noodles on tostada shells, then top with a layer of brown rice or millet. Add sautéed vegetables. Sprinkle sunflower seeds on top.

Tastes very good with miso or tofu dressing drizzled over top.

🍴 4 servings   ⏲ 20 minutes

P asta with squash sauce

1 tsp. toasted sesame oil
1 large onion, chopped
2 cups butternut squash, peeled, seeded, and cut into
  bite-sized pieces
1 tsp. sea salt
8 oz. mushrooms, sliced
1 Tbsp. shoyu
1 tsp. ginger juice, squeezed from grated ginger (optional)
8 oz. pasta, any kind

1 Heat sesame oil in large skillet. Add onion and squash and sauté briefly.

2 Add 1 teaspoon salt and water to cover bottom of pan. Lower heat, cover and simmer.

3 Add mushrooms and shoyu after about five minutes. Continue to simmer until squash is tender.

4 Add ginger juice and toss.

5 Mash until smooth. Sauce should have the consistency of mashed potatoes. If too dry, add a little water.

6 Cook pasta until tender. Rinse and drain well.

7 Serve the sauce over pasta, or use in lasagne or on pizza.

🍴 4–6 servings   ▦ 45 minutes

P asta with pumpkin sauce

8 oz. pasta, any kind
16 oz. cooked pumpkin or squash, puréed or mashed
⅓ green or red pepper, chopped
1 Tbsp. miso, any kind
1 Tbsp. mirin (optional)
1 Tbsp. shoyu
½ cup vegetable stock or water
¼ cup soy nuts or roasted sunflower seeds

1 Cook the pasta until tender.

2 While pasta is cooking, heat pumpkin in sauce pan. Add pepper and cook 5 minutes.

3 Add miso, mirin, shoyu, and as much water or stock as necessary to make sauce consistency.

4 Rinse and drain pasta.

5 Serve the sauce over pasta and garnish with soy nuts or sunflower seeds.

Pumpkin sauce is a delicious alternative to tomato sauce.

⫘ 4–6 servings   ▣ 15 minutes

F ried soba

1 pkg. soba noodles
1 Tbsp. sesame oil
1 carrot, sliced
1 celery rib, sliced

48

1½ cups cabbage, sliced
4 scallions, sliced
pinch sea salt
1½ Tbsp. ginger, minced
2 Tbsp. shoyu
2 Tbsp. mirin (optional)

1 Boil noodles until tender. Rinse, drain, and set aside to cool.

2 Heat oil and sauté vegetables one at a time beginning with those that take the longest to cook (carrot, celery, cabbage, and scallion). Add sea salt while sautéing vegetables.

3 Add ginger and sauté 1 minute. Add noodles and toss.

4 Add shoyu and mirin and toss until noodles are evenly mixed with vegetables and seasonings.

⫴ 6–8 servings   ▣ 15 minutes

N ori noodles in broth

1 pkg. soba noodles
1 strip kombu
5 cups water
3 tsp. shoyu
4 Tbsp. sesame seeds
¼ cup chopped scallions
2 sheets nori, toasted and shredded

1 Cook soba noodles. Rinse and drain well.

2 Boil kombu in 5 cups water, reduce heat to simmer

and add shoyu.

 Add sesame seeds and chopped scallions to kombu, and simmer about 10 minutes. Remove kombu.

4 Pour broth over soba noodles in bowls and sprinkle pieces of toasted nori over the top. Serve hot.

🍴 6–8 servings   ⏲ 25 minutes

Soba salad

> ½ package soba noodles, any type
> 1 large onion, sliced in thin crescents
> 1 carrot, shredded
> 1½ cups cabbage, shredded
> 1 tsp. umeboshi paste
> 1 tsp. brown-rice vinegar
> 2 Tbsp. Tofu Mayonnaise or other soy mayonnaise;
>   or tofu, boiled and mashed
> 1 tsp. shoyu
> ½ tsp. miso, any type

1 Break the soba noodles in half and cook until tender. Rinse and drain well.

2 Meanwhile, sauté onion in oil or water.

3 Combine onion, carrot, cabbage, umeboshi paste, brown-rice vinegar, soy mayonnaise or tofu, shoyu, and miso.

4 Combine the noodles and vegetable mixture.

🍴 4–6 servings   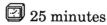 25 minutes

H ijiki noodles

½ cup hijiki, soaked, then boiled for 15 minutes
(save stock)
8 oz. noodles, any type
½ cup millet, roasted lightly
1 onion, diced
1 tsp. toasted sesame oil
Dressing:
1 cup Tofu Mayonnaise or other soy mayonnaise
2 tsp. shoyu
stock from boiling hijiki

1 Cook hijiki if not already cooked.

2 Cook noodles. Rinse and drain well.

3 Roast millet on cookie sheet at 350°F for about 5 minutes. Or dry roast in skillet over medium-low heat.

4 Sauté onion in sesame oil.

5 Add cooked hijiki to onion and continue to sauté 5 to 10 minutes.

6 Prepare dressing: Add shoyu to mayonnaise, then gradually add hijiki stock to obtain desired consistency.

7 Combine cooked noodles, sautéed onion, hijiki, and millet.

8 Add dressing to noodle mixture and toss lightly.

🍴 4–6 servings   ⏲ 30 minutes

Somen salad

    1 pkg. somen noodles
    ¼ cup sesame seeds
    1 tsp. white miso
    1 tsp. mirin (optional)
    ½ tsp. brown-rice vinegar
    ½ tsp. toasted sesame oil
    ½ bunch scallions, chopped
    1 carrot, shredded (optional)

1 Boil, drain, and cool noodles.

2 Grind sesame seeds (in suribachi or food processor), adding miso, mirin, vinegar, and toasted sesame oil to make a dressing.

3 Toss noodles and dressing together and garnish with scallions and shredded carrot if desired.

🍴 8 servings   ▦ 20 minutes

Onion noodle salad

    6 to 8 oz. noodles (any type)
    ¼ cup millet
    2 onions
Mayonnaise dressing:
    2 umeboshi plums, mashed
    1 tsp. brown-rice vinegar
    ½ cup Tofu Mayonnaise or other soy mayonnaise
    2 tsp. miso mustard

1 Cook the noodles. Rinse and drain well.

2 Roast the millet at 325°F for about 10 minutes. Or dry roast in skillet over medium-low heat.

3 Bake the onions at 325°F for 15 minutes, then chop fine. Or chop onions and sauté with or without oil.

4 Combine dressing ingredients and toss with noodles, onions, and millet.

🍴 4–6 servings   ▣ 35 minutes

N oodle burgers

> 2 cups cooked noodles, (buckwheat, whole wheat, corn, spinach)
> 1 cup cooked cereal (oatmeal, rice, corn, millet)
> ½ cup flour (any type)
> ½ tsp. sea salt
> ½ tsp. grated ginger
> ¼ cup soaked and chopped sea vegetable (nori, wakame, arame)
> oil for pan frying

1 Mix all ingredients except oil, adding a small amount of water as necessary.

2 Form patties and fry in small amount of oil about 7 minutes on each side.

Especially good served on toasted rice cakes.

🍴 4–6 servings   ▣ 20 minutes

Macaroni and cheese

2 cups macaroni or noodles (whole wheat, brown
    rice, or quinoa work well)
¼ cup millet
½ cup onion, chopped finely
½ cup broccoli, chopped
1 tsp. shoyu
2 Tbsp. Tofu Mayonnaise or other soy mayonnaise
    (optional)
½ cup soy cheese, grated
1 Tbsp. sesame seeds

1 Cook the macaroni in boiling water until tender.
Rinse and drain well.

2 Roast the millet on a cookie sheet at 350°F for about
10 minutes. Or dry roast in skillet over medium-low
heat.

3 Sauté the onion in as little water as needed to prevent sticking.

4 When onion turns golden in color, add broccoli and
shoyu and continue to sauté 5 minutes.

5 Add macaroni, soy mayonnaise if using, cheese, sesame seeds, and millet to sautéed vegetables and mix.

6 Serve, adding a touch more shoyu as desired. Or,
bake at 350°F until cheese melts.

🍴 4 servings   🖥 35 minutes

Vegetable, Grain, and Bean Dishes

R ice tempeh rolls

1 small onion, diced
1 carrot, shredded
1 tsp. miso, any type
1 cup cooked brown rice
½ cup cubed tempeh, small cubes
½ tsp. umeboshi paste
1 tsp. shoyu
4 sheets nori, toasted

1 Sauté the onion, carrot, and miso in as little water as possible, just to prevent sticking.

2 Put above ingredients in mixing bowl and add brown rice, tempeh, umeboshi paste, and shoyu. Mix well.

3 Spread ¼ of mixture evenly on each sheet of nori, leaving 1 inch uncovered at one edge, and roll up, rolling toward the uncovered edge. Moisten the 1-inch edge with water and press the roll together. Rolls will be about 2 inches across.

4 Cut each nori roll in thirds.

5 You may want to season with a little more shoyu when serving.

🍴 10–12 servings   ▨ 25 minutes

55

Bok choy salad

2 medium onions, chopped
2 large green peppers, cut in 1-inch squares
½ cup peas
½ cup celery, chopped
2 stalks bok choy, cut in 2-inch strips
2 scallions, chopped
1 to 2 tsp. shoyu
¼ cup cooked azuki beans
1 cup cooked brown rice
Mustard dressing:
¼ cup or less miso mustard
2 Tbsp. brown-rice vinegar
2 Tbsp. water

1 Sauté onions, green peppers, peas, celery, bok choy, and scallions in water and shoyu, using as little water as necessary to prevent sticking.

2 Combine dressing ingredients.

3 Mix dressing with vegetables, beans, and rice and serve warm.

¶ 4 servings 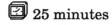 25 minutes

Assorted beans and grains

1 medium onion, chopped finely
1 carrot, chopped
2 stalks bok choy, or other greens, chopped
2 cups cooked beans (azuki, fava, kidney, white, black, or a mixture)

2 cups cooked grain (try combinations of rice, wild rice, millet, steel-cut oats, or others)
1 pkg. instant dry soup (pea, lentil, onion, or vegetable work well)

1 Pre-heat oven to 350°F.

2 Sauté vegetables; onions, carrots, and bok choy, in that order. Add a small amount of water if needed.

3 Mix beans, grain, and vegetables.

4 Add package of instant dry soup, a little water, and mix.

5 Bake at 350°F for 20 minutes.

🍴 6–8 servings   ▦ 40 minutes

Garbanzo tostada

2 tostada or tortilla shells
½ cup cooked and mashed garbanzo beans
¼ cup sautéed onions
¼ cup cabbage, shredded
¼ cup soy cheese, shredded (optional)

1 Spread the mashed garbanzo beans on tostada or tortilla shells.

2 Sprinkle onions, cabbage, and soy cheese on top.

3 Heat in 350°F oven until cheese melts.

🍴 2 servings   ▦ 10 minutes

Millet casserole

1 lb. tofu, cut in ½-inch cubes
2 tsp. shoyu
½ cup water
1⅓ cups millet
1 Tbsp. sesame oil
3 cups water
1 medium onion, sliced
8 oz. mushrooms, sliced
1 cup celery, chopped
⅔ cup parsley, chopped
1 tsp. sage
½ cup tahini
½ lb. soy cheese, grated

1 Marinate tofu in shoyu and ½ cup water for 15 minutes.

2 Sauté millet in sesame oil.

3 Add 3 cups water and simmer 20 minutes.

4 Preheat oven to 350°F.

5 Add tofu, onion, mushrooms, celery, parsley, and sage to millet. Cook 10 more minutes.

6 Add tahini and stir gently to blend.

7 Put mixture in casserole dish, adding soy cheese.

8 Bake 10 minutes at 350°F.

🍴 4 servings   ⏲ 50 minutes

N oodle bean squash casserole

 1 medium butternut squash, cut in half, seeds removed
 6 to 8 oz. udon or soba noodles
 1 large onion, chopped
 ½ cup arame seaweed, soaked and drained
 ½ cup water
 1 Tbsp. rice miso
 1 tsp. mirin (optional)
 ½ cup of water
 2 tsp. shoyu
 1 cup cooked azuki beans

1 Bake squash at 350°F for about 1 hour or until done.

2 Cook noodles, drain and rinse.

3 Sauté onion and seaweed for about 5 minutes.

4 Puree squash in blender with ½ cup water for one minute.

5 Add onion mixture, miso, and mirin to squash with ½ cup water and blend for 30 seconds.

6 Add shoyu to azuki beans and mix.

7 In an 8" x 10" baking dish, layer noodles, beans, and squash mixture.

8 Bake at 350°F for 15 minutes.

4–6 servings   90 minutes

Tempeh noodle salad

1 pkg. tempeh
1 pkg. udon noodles (8.8 oz.)
4 green onions
1 tsp. salt
2 carrots
10 small broccoli flowerettes
2 to 3 Tbsp. umeboshi plum paste
chopped parsley for garnish

1 Bake tempeh in oven at 350°F until brown on both sides or pan fry in skillet with a small amount of oil.

2 Boil 6 cups water in large pot. Drop in udon noodles.

3 Bring water back to boil and add 1 cup cold water. Repeat 2 more times. Rinse noodles in cold water. Drain well and place in a bowl.

4 Finely chop 4 green onions using both white and green portions.

5 Cut carrots in matchsticks and blanch in boiling water with 1 teaspoon salt added.

6 Remove carrots and blanch broccoli in same water.

7 Slice baked tempeh into julienne strips.

8 Combine all ingredients except umeboshi plum paste and parsley.

9 To umeboshi paste add enough water to make it creamy. Pour over salad and garnish with parsley.

6–8 servings   40 minutes

Tempeh stroganoff

¼ cup shoyu
4 Tbsp. oil
2 Tbsp. apple-cider or brown-rice vinegar
1 lb. tempeh, diced finely
¼ tsp. cumin (optional)
½ lb. mushrooms, chopped
¼ tsp. black pepper
3 Tbsp. flour
1 Tbsp. corn oil
¾ to 1 cup vegetable broth or soy milk
1 cup soygurt
8 oz. noodles

1 Make marinade of shoyu, 2 Tbsp. oil, and vinegar. Marinate the tempeh for at least 1 hour. Drain tempeh and reserve marinade.

2 Sauté tempeh in 2 Tbsp. oil in skillet until browned, then add cumin, mushrooms, pepper, and reserved marinade.

3 In a saucepan, stir flour into oil with a whisk. Add broth or soy milk and stir until thick over low heat.

4 Add sauce to tempeh. Simmer for 15 to 20 minutes over low heat, stirring occasionally. Add ¾ cup soygurt. Simmer until heated through.

5 Cook noodles, rinse and drain.

6 Serve tempeh sauce over noodles and garnish with ¼ cup soygurt.

🍴 6–8 servings   ▣ 90 minutes

P izza

1 tsp. toasted sesame oil
¾ cup onions, minced
¾ cup parsnips, cut in large slices
2 carrots, cut in large slices
½ cup broccoli, cut into medium-sized pieces
½ cup water
pinch sea salt
¼ cup brown-rice miso
1 tsp. ginger juice or grated ginger
½ cup scallions, sliced
1 cup tofu, cubed (herbed tofu is excellent)
Brown Rice Pizza Crust or other whole grain crust

1 Using 1 teaspoon sesame oil, sauté vegetables in pressure cooker or heavy skillet in following order: onions, parsnips, carrots, and broccoli. Add water and a pinch of salt.

2 If using pressure cooker, bring to pressure. Then lower temperature and cook for 15 minutes. If using a skillet, bring to a boil. Cover and cook over low heat 20 minutes or until vegetables are tender.

3 Puree vegetables; combine with miso and ginger.

4 Heat skillet, brush with oil and sauté scallions. Mix with pureed vegetables.

5 Spread puree over pizza crust, top with tofu and bake at 350°F for about 40 minutes.

Try sprinkling a small amount of soy cheese on top.

🍴 8 servings   📟 70 minutes

Roasted millet tostada

¼ cup hijiki
¾ cup millet
½ cup onion, chopped
1 Tbsp. oil or water
½ tsp. shoyu
4 tostada shells
1 cup hummus or other bean spread
½ cup soy cheese, shredded

1 Soak hijiki in water to cover for 15 minutes, then drain.

2 Wash millet and dry roast in a skillet or on a cookie sheet in oven at 350°F.

3 Sauté onion, hijiki, and millet with oil or water.

4 Add shoyu and cook 5 minutes over medium heat.

5 Heat tostada shells in 350°F oven for 3 minutes.

6 Spread hummus or bean spread on tostadas.

7 Top with millet mixture, then soy cheese.

8 Broil, just until cheese melts.

¶ 4 servings 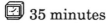 35 minutes

Accompaniments
Dressings

A masake salad dressing

> 1 cup plain amasake
> ½ cup Tofu Mayonnaise or other soy mayonnaise
> 2 Tbsp. rice vinegar
> 1 Tbsp. miso (red or brown-rice work well)
> 1 clove garlic

1 Blend the ingredients together until smooth.

2 Dress salad.

H ijiki salad dressing

> ¼ cup hijiki
> 1½ cups water
> 1 cup Tofu Mayonnaise or other soy mayonnaise
> 2 tsp. umeboshi vinegar
> 1 tsp. toasted sesame oil

1 Soak hijiki in water for 5 minutes.

2 Boil hijiki in soaking water 15 minutes, and cool. Drain and reserve liquid.

3 Mix together mayonnaise, umeboshi vinegar, and sesame oil.

4 Add hijiki to mixture. Add about ⅓ cup of reserved hijiki cooking liquid to achieve desired consistency.

P oppy seed dressing

½ Tbsp. agar agar flakes, or ¼ bar agar agar
⅔ cup water
1 cup soy milk
2 Tbsp. roasted sesame oil
1 Tbsp. brown-rice vinegar
1 clove garlic, pressed
2 tsp. poppy seeds

1 Simmer the agar agar and water in a saucepan until dissolved (5 to 8 minutes).

2 Blend the agar agar mixture and soy milk.

3 Add all other ingredients except poppy seeds and blend.

4 Add poppy seeds and stir well.

5 Chill for about one hour before serving.

U meboshi sage dressing

4 medium umeboshi plums, pitted
¼ cup water
2 tsp. toasted sesame oil
1 medium onion, minced
1 tsp. dried sage
2 scallions, chopped finely

1 Mash umeboshi plums in the water.

2 Add other ingredients and mix well.

Especially good on cooked or raw vegetables.

66

T ofu mayonnaise

1½ cups soft tofu, boiled in salted water and cooled
2 tsp. onion, minced
½ tsp. garlic, minced
2 tsp. lemon juice
½ tsp. sea salt
¼ cup water
1 to 2 tsp. shoyu

1 Blend ingredients until smooth.

Vary the taste by omitting the shoyu and adding 1 table-spoon tahini.

Sauces

S weet brown rice "cheesy" sauce

1 cup pressure-cooked sweet brown rice
1½ cups soy milk
2 tsp. miso (barley or millet work well)
1 clove garlic, minced
1 tsp. oregano (optional)

1 Combine sweet brown rice, soy milk, miso, garlic, and oregano, if using, in small saucepan.

2 Simmer over medium heat until mixture blends into a cheesy sauce.

3 Spoon sauce over pizza or casseroles, and bake for about 10 minutes. Or serve over vegetables, especially broccoli or cauliflower.

Miso tahini sauce

½ cup tahini
2 Tbsp. white miso
1 Tbsp. vinegar (rice or umeboshi)
2 scallions, chopped

1 Blend the tahini and miso.

2 Add vinegar and chopped scallions.

3 Serve with salad or over noodles.

Miso onion sauce

2 large onions, diced finely
1 to 2 Tbsp. tahini
2 Tbsp. shoyu
8 oz. tempeh cut into small cubes, for a thicker,
more hearty sauce (optional)
1 Tbsp. brown-rice miso
2 to 3 cups water

1 Simmer onions in ¼ cup water over medium heat for about 10 minutes, stirring occasionally.

2 Mix tahini with ½ cup water and add to the onion mixture.

3 Add shoyu, 1½ cups water, and tempeh, if using, to the onion sauce.

4 Simmer mixture over medium heat for approximately 30 minutes.

5 Add the miso and as much water as necessary to reach desired consistency.

6 Serve over noodles, rice, or any other grain.

Vegetable sauce

1 cup peas
kernels cut from 2 ears of corn
1½ cups onion, diced
2 medium carrots, diced
1 cup broccoli, diced
1 green pepper, diced
1 to 2 cups water
1 to 2 Tbsp. shoyu
1 Tbsp. miso
1 tsp. sea salt
½ tsp. black pepper
fresh herbs in season (optional)

1 Steam the vegetables until soft. Reserve the cooking water.

2 Puree the vegetables in a food processor or blender, using enough of the reserved water to obtain the desired consistency.

3 Reheat adding flavorings, spices, and any additional herbs as desired.

4 Serve over grain or noodles or use as pizza sauce. Or add water and serve as a creamy soup.

S oy milk sauce

1 cup soy milk
1 Tbsp. oil
1 Tbsp. kuzu or arrowroot dissolved in ⅓ cup water
1 tsp. mirin (optional)
1 Tbsp. lemon juice
1 Tbsp. shoyu

1 Combine soy milk, oil, and dissolved kuzu.

2 Simmer 3 to 5 minutes, stirring continually until mixture becomes thick.

3 Add mirin, lemon juice, and shoyu.

4 Pour over hot vegetables, fish, tempeh, or tofu.

Using toasted sesame oil will add a very special flavor.

E gg roll sauce

1 Tbsp. miso, any type
1 cup Tofu Mayonnaise or other soy mayonnaise
1 to 3 tsp. brown-rice vinegar
1 tsp. shoyu
¼ cup water (approximately)

1 Combine ingredients adding water to achieve desired consistency.

2 Serve over egg rolls.

White sauce

1 Tbsp. oil
1½ Tbsp. brown-rice flour
1½ cups soy milk
¼ tsp. sea salt
2 cloves garlic, pressed
2 tsp. mirin (optional)
chopped parsley for garnish

1 Mix oil and flour in heavy saucepan.

2 Cook over low heat, stirring constantly.

3 After 3 to 5 minutes add soy milk and continue to stir as mixture thickens.

4 Add salt, garlic, and mirin.

5 Simmer over low heat, uncovered, for about 15 minutes.

6 Remove from heat and stir in parsley.

7 Serve over cooked noodles of any type.

Spreads

Bean sandwich spread

2 cups cooked beans (garbanzos or azukis work well)
⅔ cup onion, chopped
⅓ cup peanut butter
1 Tbsp. miso
1 Tbsp. lemon juice

1 Blend the beans.

2 Add remaining ingredients mixing well. Adjust the amount of lemon juice to obtain spreadable consistency.

Makes about 1½ cups.

M iso tahini spread

1 Tbsp. onion, grated
1 clove garlic, minced
1 tsp. toasted sesame oil
½ tsp. basil (optional)
½ tsp. oregano (optional)
½ tsp. thyme or marjoram (optional)
½ cup tahini
1 Tbsp. miso (any type)
¼ to ½ cup water

1 Sauté onion and garlic in toasted sesame oil until onion becomes transparent.

2 If using, add basil, oregano, and thyme or marjoram and continue to sauté for 2 minutes.

3 Blend in tahini and sauté until mixture turns golden in color, about 7 or 8 minutes.

4 Set aside and cool until lukewarm.

5 Dilute miso in water and stir into lukewarm tahini mixture until evenly distributed.

6 Serve on breads, muffins, or crackers.

Tahini tofu spread

½ lb. tofu, boiled in salted water and cooled
⅓ cup tahini
1 to 1½ Tbsp. shoyu
½ tsp. lemon juice
1 Tbsp. onion, minced
garlic, to taste
1 stalk celery, chopped (optional)
¼ cup green pepper, chopped (optional)
½ cup alfalfa sprouts (optional)

1 Mash tofu and combine with tahini, shoyu, lemon juice, onion, and garlic, adjusting tahini and shoyu to taste.

2 Add any or all of the optional vegetables, if desired.

Bread and Pie Crust

Sprouted bread

2 cups sprouted wheat or rye
½ cup onions, finely chopped
½ cup carrots, finely chopped
¼ tsp. sea salt
¼ to ½ cup sesame seeds

1 Blend wheat or rye sprouts in blender.

2 Sauté onions and carrots in water for 3 to 5 minutes.

3 Add vegetables and salt to sprouts and blend.

4 Place on lightly-oiled cookie sheet and shape to about 1 inch thick.

5 Top with sesame seeds.

6 Bake at 150°F for about 3 hours.

Raisin nut sprouted bread

2 cups sprouted wheat or rye
¼ cup sweetener (brown-rice syrup or barley malt)
¼ cup nuts (any kind)
¼ cup raisins

1 Blend sprouts in blender or food processor.

2 Combine sprouts with remaining ingredients.

3 Shape dough into a ball and place on oiled cookie sheet.

4 Pat loaf down until it is about 1 inch thick.

5 Bake at 150°F for about 3 hours.

Brown rice pie crust

2 cups brown-rice flour
⅓ cup oil or less
½ tsp. sea salt
¼ cup sesame seeds
10 Tbsp. water (approx.)

1 Mix oil with flour and salt.

2 Add sesame seeds and as little water as necessary to form dough into ball. Handle dough gently so crust will be tender.

3 Cut dough into two parts. One at a time, place dough between two sheets of waxed paper and roll with rolling pin.

4 Flip each into an 8-inch pie pan by removing top sheet of waxed paper and flipping waxed paper with rolled pie dough over pan. Peel off waxed paper. Using hands, smooth out dough, and bake at 400°F for 5 to 10 minutes. Or, before baking, fill with desired filling and follow filling recipe for baking instructions.

Brown rice pizza crust

     1 cup brown-rice flour
     1 cup cooked brown rice
     3 to 6 Tbsp. oil
     ½ tsp. sea salt
     ⅓ cup sunflower seeds, roasted
     10 Tbsp. water (approx.)

1 Mix oil with flour, rice, and salt.

2 Add sunflower seeds and as little water as needed to form dough into ball.

3 Press dough into pizza pans, cover with topping and bake at 400°F for about 20 minutes. Or divide dough in two parts, roll each between two sheets of waxed paper with a rolling pin and use as pie crust.

Easy press-in pie crust

1½ cups corn flour
¼ tsp. cinnamon
¼ cup water or apple juice
2 Tbsp. millet, roasted or raw

1 Combine flour and cinnamon.

2 Add water or apple juice gradually, making sure mixture doesn't become too wet. Gently mix or knead.

3 Press the dough into a pie pan with your hands. It works best to form the dough into a ball and then flatten it out into the pan.

4 Sprinkle the millet over the top of the crust and press lightly. Bake at 350°F for about 7 to 10 minutes. Or before baking, fill and bake as directed in the filling recipe.

Desserts and Snacks
Cookies, Cakes, and Muffins

Sunnie carob cookies

¼ cup tahini
⅓ cup brown-rice syrup
⅓ cup tofu, mashed
¼ cup carob powder
½ cup brown-rice flour
3 Tbsp. soy flour (optional; use brown-rice flour or corn flour instead)
⅓ cup whole-wheat flour
¼ cup walnuts, roasted

1 Preheat oven to 350°F.

2 Cream together tahini and brown-rice syrup.

3 Add tofu and blend well.

4 Slowly add carob powder a little at a time. When all is added, beat vigorously.

5 Combine rice flour and soy flour. Then add wheat flour.

6 Mix flour and carob mixture, adding walnuts.

7 Roll dough into small balls and flatten into 1½-inch rounds on unoiled cookie sheet.

8 Bake about 15 minutes. Cool on rack.

🍴 3 to 4 dozen cookies.

lfalfa sprout cookies

1 cup flour (rice, corn, or whole-wheat)
⅛ cup sesame seeds
½ cup nut butter (peanut, sesame, almond, or sun-
    flower)
¼ cup concentrated sweetener (barley malt or
    brown-rice syrup)
1 Tbsp. molasses (optional)
1 tsp. vanilla (optional)
2 carrots, grated
¼ cup alfalfa sprouts

1 Preheat oven to 350°F.

2 Combine the dry ingredients.

3 Combine nut butter, concentrated sweetener, molasses, and vanilla, if using, in pan over low heat.

4 Remove pan from stove and add grated carrots and
alfalfa sprouts.

5 Add dry ingredients to form dough.

6 Form heaping tablespoons of dough into round ball
shapes and flatten onto oiled cookie sheet.

7 Bake at 350°F for about 8 to 10 minutes until lightly
browned.

For Carob Chip Cookies, add 1 cup unsweetened, non-
dairy carob chips with the grated carrots. Also, try using
other types of sprouts.

🍴 18 to 20 cookies.

Miso carob chip cookies

¼ cup tahini
2 Tbsp. brown-rice miso
⅓ cup brown-rice syrup
2 Tbsp. amasake (optional)
⅓ cup tofu, mashed
¼ cup carob powder
½ cup brown-rice flour
3 Tbsp. soy flour (optional; use more brown-rice flour
  instead)
⅓ cup whole-wheat flour
¼ cup sunflower seeds
¼ cup unsweetened, non-dairy carob chips

1 Preheat oven to 350°F.

2 Cream together tahini, miso, brown-rice syrup, and amasake, if using.

3 Add tofu and blend well.

4 Slowly add carob powder a little at a time. When all is added, beat vigorously.

5 Combine rice flour and soy flour, then add wheat flour.

6 Mix flour with carob mixture, adding sunflower seeds and carob chips.

7 Roll dough into small balls and flatten into 2½-inch rounds on unoiled cookie sheets.

8 Bake about 15 minutes. Cool on rack.

🍴 3 to 4 dozen cookies.

Mugwort mochi cookies

½ cup mugwort mochi, shredded
½ cup brown-rice flour
½ cup whole-grain cereal (any kind)
¼ cup roasted millet
2 Tbsp. tahini
¼ to ½ cup apple juice or amasake
¼ cup brown-rice syrup
1 tsp. vanilla
2 Tbsp. kuzu dissolved in 2 Tbsp. water
½ cup unsweetened, non-dairy carob chips

1 Preheat oven to 350°F.

2 Mix together the grated mochi, flour, cereal, and millet.

3 In saucepan, heat tahini, ¼ cup apple juice or amasake, brown-rice syrup, and vanilla.

4 Add kuzu and water to tahini mixture.

5 Mix wet ingredients with dry ingredients, adjusting amount of apple juice or amasake to obtain desired consistency.

6 Add carob chips.

7 Form into cookies. Press onto lightly-oiled cookie sheet and bake at 350°F for 10 to 12 minutes.

🍴 16 to 20 cookies.

O atmeal cookies

½ cup brown-rice-syrup powder
1½ cups brown-rice flour
2 cups rolled oats
1 tsp. sea salt
½ cup nuts, chopped (walnuts, almonds, or pecans)
2 Tbsp. oil
1 cup water, juice, or amasake
1 tsp. vanilla

1 Preheat oven to 350°F.

2 Mix dry ingredients in a bowl.

3 Blend oil, water, juice, or amasake, and vanilla.

4 Mix dry ingredients with wet ingredients just until moist.

5 Spoon cookies onto well-oiled cookie sheet and bake for about 20 minutes, until lightly browned.

¶ 2 dozen cookies.

P uffed millet cookies

¾ cup amasake
½ cup brown-rice flour
½ cup puffed millet, or other ready-to-eat cereal
¼ cup sunflower seeds
½ tsp. vanilla
¼ cup walnuts
½ cup unsweetened, non-dairy carob chips

1 Preheat oven to 350°F.

2 Combine amasake, brown-rice flour, and puffed millet or other cereal.

3 Add sunflower seeds, vanilla, walnuts, and carob chips and mix.

4 Lightly oil cookie sheet, if desired. Spoon dough on to cookie sheet and bake at 350°F for about 12 minutes.

🍴 12 to 15 cookies.

Raisin cookies

½ cup brown-rice-syrup powder
1½ cups brown-rice flour
2 cups rolled oats
1 tsp. sea salt
¾ cup raisins
½ cup walnuts, almonds, or pecans, chopped (optional)
1 tsp. cinnamon (optional)
2 Tbsp. oil
1 cup water or juice
1 tsp. vanilla

1 Preheat oven to 350°F.

2 Mix dry ingredients and raisins in a bowl.

3 Blend oil, water or juice, and vanilla.

4 Mix dry ingredients with wet ingredients just until moist.

5 Spoon cookies onto well-oiled cookie sheet and bake

for about 20 minutes, or until lightly browned.

🍴 2 dozen cookies.

R eunion cookies

> ¼ cup peanut butter
> ¼ cup sesame tahini
> 1 tsp. vanilla
> ½ cup concentrated sweetener (brown-rice syrup, barley malt, fruit juice)
> 2 cups rolled oats, roasted
> 1 cup brown-rice flour
> ⅛ cup millet
> ¼ cup sunflower seeds
> ¼ cup unsweetened, non-dairy carob chips
> apple juice, as needed

1 Preheat oven to 350°F.

2 Heat peanut butter, tahini, vanilla, and concentrated sweetener in saucepan over low heat.

3 Mix dry ingredients together.

4 Combine wet and dry ingredients adding apple juice to obtain cookie-dough consistency.

5 Spoon cookies onto lightly-oiled cookie sheet and bake for approximately 12 minutes.

🍴 2 dozen cookies.

Millet crunch cookies

  1½ cups brown-rice flour
  ¾ cup rolled oats
  ¼ cup poppy seeds
  ½ cup millet
  2 Tbsp. kuzu
  ¾ cup unsweetened, non-dairy carob chips
  ½ cup raisins
  ¾ cup soy milk
  ½ cup brown-rice syrup
  1 tsp. vanilla (optional)

1 Preheat oven to 350°F.

2 Blend dry ingredients.

3 Blend liquid ingredients separately, then mix with dry ingredients until moist. Add a bit more soy milk if needed.

4 Shape dough into small balls and flatten onto light-ly-oiled cookie sheet.

5 Bake at 350°F for about 10 to 12 minutes.

🍴 2 dozen cookies.

Sweet cereal bars

  ½ cup barley malt
  1 tsp. vanilla
  pinch sea salt
  3 to 4 Tbsp. nut butter (peanut, sunflower, almond)
  1 box natural ready-to-eat cereal (wheat, rice, corn)

1 Heat the barley malt, vanilla, salt, and nut butter in a saucepan over low heat. Add about ⅓ cup water if mixture is too thick.

2 Pour barley-malt mixture over the cereal, and press into a pan or on cookie sheet.

3 Let sit until cooled and cut into bars or squares.

 masake bars

    1 cup brown-rice flour
    ½ cup rolled oats
    ½ cup whole millet or millet flour
    ¼ cup raisins
    ¼ cup unsweetened, non-dairy carob chips
    ¼ cup walnuts
    1½ cups amasake
    ⅓ to ½ cup apple juice

1 Preheat oven to 350°F.

2 Mix together dry ingredients.

3 Add amasake and mix.

4 Gradually add apple juice to obtain desired consistency.

5 Spoon into lightly-oiled 9" x 9" baking pan.

6 Bake at 350°F for about 20 minutes or until lightly browned on top.

7 Cool slightly and cut into bars or squares.

🍴 16 to 20 bars.

Corn flake bars

½ box natural corn flakes or brown-rice cereal
2 Tbsp. kuzu, powdered
½ cup brown-rice syrup
1 cup soy milk or amasake or a combination of the
    two
½ cup mixture of chopped walnuts, uncooked millet,
    and sunflower seeds
1 cup unsweetened, non-dairy carob chips

1 Preheat oven to 350°F.

2 Mix the cereal and kuzu with the brown-rice syrup
and soy milk or amasake.

3 Add the walnut-millet-seed mixture and the carob
chips.

4 Spread mixture in baking pan and bake for about 15
minutes. Cut into bars.

This dessert tastes especially good frozen.

Mochi waffle cones

2 to 3 ozs. mochi per cone (cinnamon raisin mochi or
    plain mochi)

1 Grate mochi.

2 Spread mochi into heated waffle iron in about a 4-
inch square.

3 Heat mochi until it melts together (3 to 5 minutes).

4 Remove mochi from waffle iron while flexible and shape into a cone.

5 Set cones over small cups on a cookie sheet and bake at 350°F for about 10 minutes.

pplesauce cake

> 1 cup applesauce
> ¼ cup oil
> 1 cup soy milk
> ¾ cup amasake
> 1 tsp. vanilla
> 2 Tbsp. barley malt
> 1 cup brown-rice flour
> 2 cups other flour (whole-wheat, corn, etc.)
> 2 tsp. baking powder
> 2 tsp. baking soda
> ¼ tsp. sea salt

1 Preheat oven to 375°F. Lightly oil a 10" x 14" cake pan.

2 Blend applesauce and liquid ingredients together in a blender.

3 Mix dry ingredients.

4 Pour liquid mixture into flour mixture and beat for 3 minutes.

5 Pour batter into cake pan and bake for 30 minutes.

6 When done, cool cake on cake rack and turn onto serving platter.

Top with Custard Filling and choice of fruit.

N utty carob rice cakes

½ cup millet
¼ cup brown-rice syrup
¼ cup carob powder
¼ cup walnuts, chopped
⅛ cup tahini
1 tsp. vanilla (optional)
½ tsp. anise (optional)
6 rice cakes

1 Toast millet on cookie sheet at 350°F for 10 to 12 minutes or in dry skillet over medium heat.

2 Combine brown-rice syrup, carob powder, walnuts, tahini, and vanilla or anise, if using, in saucepan. Heat until warmed.

3 Add toasted millet to saucepan and stir.

4 Dip rice cakes in saucepan, one at a time, to cover with mixture, then set on plate or waxed paper to cool.

R ice muffins

1½ cups rice flour
2 tsp. arrowroot flour
½ cup raisins or dates
¼ cup brown-rice syrup or barley malt
⅓ cup soy milk or fruit juice
¼ cup nut butter (peanut, sesame, sunflower, or almond)

1 Preheat oven to 350°F. Lightly oil muffin pan.

2 Combine flour and arrowroot in bowl.

3 Add dates or raisins.

4 In another bowl, combine brown-rice syrup or barley malt, soy milk or fruit juice, and nut butter. Mix well.

5 Add liquid ingredients to dry. Stir just until smooth.

6 Spoon batter into muffin pan until two-thirds full.

7 Bake for about 15 minutes.

Puddings, Fillings, and Frostings

 masake gelatin

1 Tbsp. kanten flakes
1 cup amasake
½ tsp. flavoring (vanilla, almond, anise, raspberry, or orange)
¼ cup nuts or seeds (sunflower, sesame, walnuts, or other)
¼ cup dried fruit (raisins, apples, dates, or other)

1 Add kanten flakes to amasake.

2 Stir and bring to a boil.

3 Reduce heat and simmer 5 minutes or until dissolved. Add flavoring.

4 Add nuts or seeds and dried fruit.

5 Pour into serving container and chill until set.

pple oatmeal pudding

1½ cups apple juice
1½ cups water
1 to 1⅓ cups rolled oats, depending on desired thick-
    ness
1 apple, sliced into small pieces
½ tsp. cinnamon
¼ cup walnuts or sunflower seeds, roasted
3 Tbsp. soy milk (optional)

1 Boil apple juice and water.

2 Add rolled oats, boil over high heat 1 to 2 minutes,
then reduce heat to medium for 5 to 7 minutes.

3 Add apple and cinnamon.

4 Cook over low heat 5 to 7 minutes, or until oats are
done.

5 Add nuts and soy milk, if using. Mix thoroughly and
serve.

C arob custard

4 cups apple juice or 3 cups apple juice and 1 cup wa-
    ter
1 Tbsp. tahini
2 Tbsp. barley malt or brown-rice syrup
1 Tbsp. carob powder
1 tsp. vanilla
2 Tbsp. kanten flakes
2 Tbsp. kuzu

1 Combine all ingredients except kanten and kuzu in a blender and blend for 1 minute.

2 Add kuzu and kanten and blend for another minute.

3 Pour in a pan and heat until boiling. Reduce heat and simmer for about 10 minutes.

4 Let the mixture cool and chill in refrigerator for about 1 hour.

5 Blend until smooth and serve as a custard or pour into a baked pie shell.

This is a very versatile dish. You can replace the carob powder with carob chips and nuts on top. Or top with fresh fruit or raisins. Add a crumb topping for an elegant dessert. Adjust the tahini and sweetener to your own personal taste.

Custard

2 Tbsp. brown-rice syrup
2 cups soy milk
1 tsp. vanilla
4 Tbsp. kuzu or arrowroot dissolved in ⅓ cup water

1 Heat brown-rice syrup, soy milk, and vanilla in saucepan over medium heat.

2 Add dissolved kuzu, turn heat to low, and stir constantly for 3 to 5 minutes until the mixture thickens.

3 Spoon into serving dishes, a baked pie shell, or serve as a sauce.

Cherry kuzu pudding

2 cups fresh cherries, pitted
¼ cup cherry juice and water
2 Tbsp. kuzu
1 Tbsp. brown-rice syrup

1 Drain cherries and reserve juice. Add water to cherry juice if needed to make ¼ cup of liquid.

2 Heat kuzu and liquid very slowly over medium heat until kuzu thickens.

3 Add sweetener and cherries and mix.

Great as a pie filling, pudding, or as a sauce over a gelled dessert. Other fruits may be used.

Oat creme

1 cup rolled oats
4 to 6 cups apple juice
¼ cup tahini
½ tsp. sea salt
¼ cup concentrated sweetener (brown-rice syrup, barley malt, or fruit juice)
4 tsp. grain coffee (optional)
1 tsp. cinnamon
1 tsp. vanilla or almond flavoring (optional)

1 Roast oats until lightly browned.

2 Combine juice, tahini, and oats in a heavy pot.

3 Add sea salt, sweetener, and grain coffee. Bring to a

boil, stirring occasionally.

4 Lower heat, cover, and simmer for 20 minutes.

5 After cooking, add cinnamon and vanilla or almond, blending until smooth.

6 Adjust liquid content until desired texture is obtained.

7 Pour into a serving dish or into a baked pie shell. Refrigerate until set.

masake frosting

    1 tsp. kanten powder or flakes
    ⅓ cups water
    ½ tsp. sea salt
    1 cup amasake
    ¼ cup brown-rice syrup or barley malt
    1 tsp. vanilla, almond, or anise flavoring

1 Add kanten powder to water. Bring to a boil and then simmer for about 15 minutes.

2 Add sea salt, amasake, and brown-rice syrup or barley malt and continue to simmer 5 more minutes.

3 Add the vanilla, almond, or anise flavoring. Remove from heat and let cool until frosting thickens to desired consistency.

4 Drizzle on cake, cookies, or bars.

Carob chip frosting

1 Tbsp. kuzu
1 cup plain amasake
¼ tsp. sea salt
¼ cup unsweetened, non-dairy carob chips
¼ tsp. vanilla, almond, or anise extract

1 In a saucepan, dissolve kuzu in amasake. Add salt.

2 Stir continuously while bringing to boil.

3 Reduce heat and simmer 20 minutes, stirring occasionally.

4 Stir in carob chips and vanilla, almond, or anise extract for flavoring.

5 After mixture is cool, frost cake or cookies.

Pies and Crisps

Apple pie

7 or 8 apples, cored and sliced (peeled if preferred)
1 tsp. cinnamon
1 Tbsp. kuzu dissolved in ¼ cup apple juice
2 Tbsp. barley malt
¼ cup raisins and/or walnuts (optional)
1 recipe Dessert Pie Crust, baked 5 min.
1 recipe Millet Crunch Topping

1 Mix apples, cinnamon, kuzu, and juice together in

large bowl.

2 Add barley malt. Add raisins and walnuts, if using.

3 Let mixture set 30 minutes for flavors to blend, then press into pie crust and top with crunch topping.

4 Bake at 350°F for 35 to 40 minutes.

pricot pie

> 2 cups apricots, sliced
> ¼ cup apple juice
> 2 tsp. kuzu, dissolved in 2 Tbsp. water
> 2 Tbsp. barley malt
> 1 tsp. cinnamon (optional)
> 1 recipe Dessert Pie Crust, baked 5 min.
> 1 recipe Millet Crunch Topping

1 Simmer the apricots in apple juice until apricots soften.

2 Add kuzu and barley malt and continue to heat until thick.

3 Add cinnamon, if using, and pour mixture into pie crust. Top with crunch topping.

4 Bake at 350°F for 30 minutes.

The amount of kuzu may be adjusted according to desired consistency.

A masake cheese pie

12 oz. soy cream cheese
16 oz. frozen amasake (any flavor)
1 tsp. vanilla
1 to 2 Tbsp. kuzu dissolved in 3 Tbsp. water
1 recipe Dessert Pie Crust, baked 12 min.

1 Blend cream cheese and amasake.

2 Add vanilla and dissolved kuzu. Mix until creamy.

3 Fill pie shell with amasake filling and refrigerate overnight or freeze for 4 to 5 hours.

Try adding fruit to the filling or top with Cherry Kuzu Pudding.

D essert pie crust

1½ Tbsp. tahini
¼ cup apple juice
1½ cups rolled oats, roasted
1 cup millet
¼ cup flour, any type

1 Melt tahini into apple juice in saucepan over medium heat.

2 Add all other ingredients to tahini mixture to make a dough.

3 Form dough into a ball. Roll out between two sheets of waxed paper with a rolling pin. Fit dough into a

9-inch pie pan.

4 Bake pie crust for about 12 minutes at 350°F. Or if pie will be baked after it is filled, bake crust for 5 minutes only.

5 Let pie crust cool before putting filling in.

If you wish to make a covered pie, double the recipe or top pie with Millet Crunch Topping.

P oppy seed apple crisp

> 6 rice cakes
> ¼ cup millet
> ¼ cup walnuts
> 8 medium apples
> 1 to 1½ cups soy milk
> ¼ cup brown-rice syrup
> 2 Tbsp. poppy seeds

1 Toast rice cakes, millet, and walnuts on cookie sheets in oven at 300°F for about 10 minutes.

2 Slice apples and cook in saucepan with soy milk, using enough soy milk to keep apples moist while cooking about 10 to 12 minutes.

3 Mix the millet, walnuts, and brown-rice syrup into the apple mixture.

4 Put mixture into a 9" x 12" baking pan and spread crumbled rice cakes over the top.

5 Sprinkle the poppy seeds over the top, then bake for 30 minutes at 350°F.

Rice apple crisp

8 apples
1 Tbsp. arrowroot flour
4 Tbsp. brown-rice syrup or barley malt
½ cup chopped walnuts, roasted
6 mochi rice cakes, crumbled

1 Slice apples into 9" x 11" baking dish and sprinkle with arrowroot.

2 Mix crumbled rice cakes and walnuts and sprinkle over apples.

3 Drizzle rice syrup or barley malt over crumbs and bake at 350°F for 30 minutes. Serve warm.

Crunchy dessert topping

½ cup millet
2 cups rolled oats
⅓ cup sunflower seeds or peanuts
⅓ cup brown-rice syrup or barley malt
¼ cup tahini or peanut butter
¼ cup fruit juice to desired consistency

1 Roast the millet and rolled oats on cookie sheet in oven at 250°F for 1 hour or in skillet over low heat until slightly browned.

2 Heat brown-rice syrup or barley malt, tahini or peanut butter, and fruit juice over low heat until ingredients are blended.

3 Mix wet ingredients and dry ingredients including sunflower seeds.

4 Roast mixture in oven at 250°F for about 30 minutes. Then cool and store in airtight container in refrigerator.

Raisins or other dried fruit, carob chips, or nuts may be added to mixture after it is cool.

Millet crunch topping

    ¾ cup rolled oats
    2 Tbsp. sunflower seeds or walnuts
    ¼ cup millet
    ¼ cup brown-rice flour
    2 Tbsp. brown-rice syrup or barley malt
    2 Tbsp. soy milk

1 In a 350°F oven, roast oats until lightly browned, about 30 minutes. Roast sunflower seeds or walnuts and millet about 10 minutes.

2 Mix dry ingredients together, adding sweetener and soy milk.

3 Place mixture over pie filling or over fruit to make a crisp. Or use in place of a top crust for a covered pie. Bake as directed in pie or crisp recipe.

Snacks and Beverages

Rice cakes

2 cups cooked brown rice (sweet rice works best)
¼ cup any other grain such as millet, couscous, quinoa, barley, oats, wild rice (optional)
1 tsp. miso or 1 tsp. shoyu or 1 tsp. umeboshi paste or 1 to 2 tsp. tahini
¼ cup sesame seeds or ⅛ to ¼ cup sunflower seeds, roasted

1 If not already cooked, cook the brown rice in pressure cooker or saucepan until done. If using one of the optional grains, substitute this for part of the brown rice, and cook with the brown rice. Rice cakes work best if the rice is rather moist.

2 While rice is still hot, mix in miso, shoyu, umeboshi, or tahini and sesame seeds or sunflower seeds.

3 Let mixture cool.

4 Preheat oven to 350°F.

5 Form patties from the rice mixture, about the size of rice cakes, and place on cookie sheet.

6 Bake at 350°F for about 10 to 15 minutes on each side. Flip the rice cakes over with a spatula.

These rice cakes are very chewy.

Carob rice balls

½ cup millet
1½ to 2 Tbsp. tahini or other seed or nut butter (peanut, sunflower, almond, etc.)
¼ cup barley malt
1 cup cooked sweet brown rice
¼ cup nuts or seeds (any type)
½ cup unsweetened, non-dairy carob chips
1 tsp. vanilla (optional)

1 Roast the millet in oven at 350°F for about 5 minutes or in dry skillet over medium heat.

2 Warm the tahini and barley malt in a saucepan over
low heat until creamy.

3 Combine all ingredients, shape into balls and refrigerate until set.

Great for traveling.

Baked skins

leftover squash or potato skins
shoyu
sesame seeds
nori, toasted and crumbled (optional)

1 After baking, remove squash or potato from skins.

2 Brush skins with shoyu and sprinkle with sesame
seeds and nori.

3 Bake for 5 minutes until crispy.

P eanut butter popcorn

½ cup unpopped popcorn
2 Tbsp. barley malt
1½ Tbsp. peanut butter
1 or 2 Tbsp. apple juice
½ cup walnuts or sunflower seeds, roasted
¼ cup raisins
2 sheets nori

1 Pop popcorn and set aside.

2 Heat barley malt, peanut butter, and apple juice over low heat until mixture melts.

3 Pour liquid over popcorn and mix.

4 Add roasted nuts or seeds and raisins, mixing again.

5 Roast nori in oven at 350°F for about 30 seconds or over burner (watch carefully as it burns easily). When roasted cut or tear into small pieces and sprinkle over top.

Try adding sliced apples, fresh or dried.

M ovie snack

3 cups popcorn, measured after popping
3 rice cakes
½ cup mixture of walnuts, roasted and chopped, raisins, unsweetened carob chips, sunflower seeds, pumpkin seeds (use any or all)
vegetable seasoning (optional)

1 sheet nori (optional)
¼ to ½ cup soy cheese, shredded (optional)

1 Pop the popcorn.

2 Warm the rice cakes in oven at 350°F, then break them into small pieces and mix with the popcorn.

3 Add the ½ cup of nut-seed-fruit mixture. Sprinkle vegetable seasoning of your choice over the top.

4 If using nori, toast the nori at 350°F for about 10 to 15 seconds or over a burner until sheet turns green. Shred the nori with your hands and mix with other ingredients.

5 Add soy cheese if desired.

Amasake fruit drink

1 cup plain amasake
1 Tbsp. sesame tahini
1 to 1½ cups fresh fruit
¼ to ½ cup water, boiled with ¼ tsp. salt and cooled

1 Blend ingredients together, using ¼ cup water and adjusting the amount of fruit to desired sweetness and consistency.

2 Add more water if needed.

Ginger amasake drink

1 cup amasake, any flavor
¾ cup water
pinch sea salt
½ tsp. ginger, grated

1 Bring amasake to a boil with water and salt.

2 Remove from heat and add ginger.

3 Serve like traditional cocoa.

Ethnic Dinners

We began having much fun creating new and different taste sensations. Our enthusiasm was hard to contain, so we began sharing our meals by creating a natural-foods cooking center and sponsoring both dinners and classes. We have also had guest lecturers teach classes and guest cooks prepare dinners. The ethnic dinners are now attended very well twice a month. Each dinner has a different cuisine.

Although all of the dinners are "mostly macrobiotic" and use no animal products, they are advertised by their nationality. Some typical dinners are outlined here and we do try many variations. We find that it is a lot of fun to take an ethnic recipe and "healthify" it using more wholesome products.

Menus for Ethnic Dinners

Japanese
Squash Pie
Stuffed Nori
Onion Noodle Salad
Custard

Spinach Fried Tofu
Fried Soba
Nutty Rice Salad
Amasake Bars

Italian
Pizza (appetizers)
Lasagne with Squash Sauce
Corn Salad
Applesauce Cake

Chinese

Vegetable Pancakes
Millet Egg Rolls
Fried Rice
Bok Choy Salad
Rice Muffins

Green Pea Rice
Oriental Coleslaw
Squash Pie
Custard in Dessert Pie Crust

Middle Eastern

White Sauce over noodles
Millet Salad
Rice Muffins with Miso Tahini Spread
Miso Carob Chip Cookies

Greek

Baked Cabbage Bundles
Simple, Elegant Swiss Chard in pie shell
Nutty Rice Salad
Millet Crunch Cookies

Mexican

Green Pea Rice
Hijiki Salad
Sea Vegie Tostada
Corn Flake Bars

American Vegetarian

Tempeh Stroganoff
Broccoli with Miso Onion Sauce
Brown Rice Salad
Millet Crunch Cookies with Amasake Frosting

Tofu au Gratin
Nori Noodles in Broth
Soba Salad
Millet Salad
Applesauce Cake

Travel Made Simple

Traveling can make adherance to a healthy diet difficult. Ideas for equipment and staples can help to simpli-
fy the process of leaving home. We have found that for
cooking on the road, whether it be on a camping trip or
in a fancy hotel, our basic procedure is the same. With a
very simple equipment list and a few dried foods, we
have managed to fix simple, elegant meals. Often we
will supplement our supplies with locally-grown vegetables.

Getting used to this whole process has taken some
adjusting. We travelled to the Pocono Mountains with
our son Jacob when he was about nine months old. We
had some emergency "rest stop" meals in which we
quickly cooked up a batch of cereal including vegetables
as Jacob loudly complained. We soon learned to save
some cereal from the prior meal for between-meal
snacks.

As an example of the process used to prepare for a
trip, here's a list of supplies for a four-day trip for two.

Suggested Equipment:

single-burner camp stove
one-quart stainless-steel saucepan with lid
small frying pan for sautéing
small paring knife
small wooden cutting board
ginger grater
wooden stirring spoon
bottle for bancha tea
small plastic bags
two small bowls

two tea cups
chopsticks
soup spoons
napkins
sponge stored in plastic bag for cleaning dishes
dish towels
additions: two plates, a larger bowl, sushi mat, and
rice paddles may all be added if room is available.

Staple Foods:

pre-packaged brown-rice dinners
rolled oats
ramen and other noodles
dry miso soup
small bag of sea vegetables (combinations of kombu,
wakame, arame, and nori)
mushrooms
sesame seeds
3 Tbsp. miso
small bottle soy sauce
4 umeboshi
1 Tbsp. umeboshi paste
ginger
1 oz. bottle sesame oil
bancha tea bags

These items fit quite nicely into a "gym" type bag.
Whether camping out or staying in a motel, we just add
fresh vegetables when possible and enjoy elegant meals.

Cooking Tips:

1. Cook grain first, as it takes the longest.
2. Try pan frying or roasting the grain before cooking
to bring out flavor.
3. Place vegetables in pan with small amount of water and heat until vegetables become tender.

4. Make the soup last using leftover liquids from the vegetables.

Travel Recipe Ideas:

Parboiled Rice
Parboiled Millet
Pre-cooked Tofu
Rice Vegie Pilaf
Fried Rice
Green Pea Rice
Stuffed Nori
Arame Oatmeal
Oatmeal with Fall Vegetables
Carob Rice Balls

Transition
Pam's Experience

Before I became interested in macrobiotics I had been involved in major dietary changes over a period of eight or nine years. I had gradually reduced meat and sugar in the first two to three years. From that point I began reducing my intake of dairy products more and more until I no longer had a desire for them. This took four or five years.

Eating alone has been part of my struggle to treat myself well. It has always been so much easier to skip a meal or just eat whatever is around rather than create a well balanced and great tasting dish just for me.

Changing the "meat" of my diet was very challenging, especially since the only vegetables I would eat were corn and green beans. I began this process while attending graduate school. Instead of taking away all of the meat I began by gradually adding a greater quantity and variety of vegetables. I used personal commitment as my avenue to change, deciding that once a week I would buy a new vegetable (remember that most of them were new to me). I would ask someone how to cook it, and I would use this new vegetable in a dish.

I still remember the first week. I marched into the farmers' market with all the confidence I could muster and picked out a purple and oval shaped vegetable. Then I approached an older woman who looked like she might be a well-seasoned cook and asked, "What is this called?" Her reply was, "An eggplant, of course," as if to say, "Don't you *know* what an eggplant is?"

I then asked, "And how do I cook with this eggplant?"

At this point she began to recite a complex recipe for Eggplant Parmesan. I listened intently for a few minutes until I was totally overwhelmed. Then when I could stand it no more I quickly blurted out that I appreciated her help but I was not ready for her plan for eggplant. As I left I decided that I would find a simpler and easier way to make that eggplant taste good.

Gradually I came to know and like many vegetables. I found the proportions of the meals I prepared gradually changing: more vegetables and less and less meat and dairy products.

Another major shift in cooking and eating for me occurred when I began to substitute more soy products in place of the familiar dairy products I had eaten for so long. I discovered how easily I could substitute a smaller amount of soy cheese and tofu in recipes.

I had and still have a very difficult time giving up sweets. This process is ongoing. I finally came to face my sugar addiction, shortly after returning to graduate school about twelve years ago. All my life I had liked sweets and had eaten more than my share of candy and birthday cakes. It wasn't until age 26 that I chose to begin the process of letting go of sugar.

I read the book *Sugar Blues* by William Dufty.

I began studying nutrition in my course work.

I made the realization of the power that sugar had over me.

I made a series of commitments that I would no longer buy cookies, cakes, or other desserts. If I were to eat desserts, I would make them from scratch. This helped tremendously since I had very little time to bake or prepare them.

I started out by making cakes or cookies now and

then using about half the amount of sugar required and gradually adding more and more healthful ingredients: seeds, nuts, wheat, rice or oat bran, dried fruits, etc. As I discovered new and different sweeteners to use, I became more and more motivated to eat less. The shift went from sugar to honey, gradually reducing the amount of honey used. From honey I shifted to the use of very small amounts of maple syrup and/or fruit juice, particularly apple juice. When I began to study macrobiotics I discovered brown rice syrup and barley malt and once again changed. Not only did I use fewer sweeteners in my desserts; I also found my need and desire for sweets dramatically changing.

These processes freed me in the realization that I could alter recipes and still make them taste good. Soon I was creating my own recipes from scratch and coming up with all kinds of new concoctions. Recipes for lunches and dinners evolved and gave me a terrific sense of creativity and bolstered my self-esteem.

Lee's Experience

In the last five years I have relearned something I don't like to admit: I have a hard time changing. Whether it be something as momentous as getting married at age 35, eating brown rice instead of bratwurst, or learning to share my feelings — change is hard for me. For much of my life I hassled myself about this fact. Only in the last two years have I been able to accept this part of me. Who knows — in two more years I may even be able to laugh at it. Now that would be a big change!

In the last five years, with the guidance, help, and

most important, friendship, of my wife and others, I have been slowly changing what I eat. It has been exciting. I have enjoyed eating new foods and discovering how wonderful vegetables and brown rice can taste. I have also enjoyed the new energy this has brought me. I have enjoyed the new people I have met in the Pocono Mountains, at French Meadows, and at other places as I have explored the world of macrobiotics. However, there has been a backdoor to this change. I have struggled to let go of my early eating patterns, and even more difficult, I have struggled to let go of my old thinking patterns and ways of behaving which limit my growth.

I met two delightful people at a conference in the Pocono Mountains. What struck me about them was their ability to laugh at their humaness and about their macrobiotic diet. They told a story of the concern of the hostess at a barbecue that they wouldn't have enough to eat since they didn't eat meat. They responded that if they were still hungry, they could always go into the backyard and graze a little!

I want to put more laughter in my life and laugh at my resistance to change instead of getting uptight about it. Macrobiotics has helped me see that I have a lot of change left in my life and that I might just as well sit back, laugh, and enjoy the process.

Cravings

We found that as we began making major eating-habit changes, cravings for the "old foods" surfaced. One of our ways of dealing with this was to just Have Some. Another was to substitute other foods for the particular item craved. The following list gives you example recipes to try when a particular craving comes your way. You can gain ideas by trying these and then go on to create your own concoctions.

Dairy-Product Cravings:

Amasake Salad Dressing
Tofu au Gratin
Pizza
Tofu Mayonnaise
Tahini Tofu Spread
Oat Creme Pie
Amasake Frosting
Ginger Amasake Drink
Miso Tahini Sauce

Meat/Animal-Food Cravings:

Tempeh Noodle Salad
Sunnie Burgers
Noodle Burgers
Oat Burgers
Spinach Fried Tofu
Rice Tempeh Rolls
Bean Sandwich Spread
Tofu au Gratin

Sweet Cravings:

Carob Chip Frosting
Oat Creme Pie
Alfalfa Sprout Cookies
Poppy Seed Apple Crisp
Sunny Carob Cookies
Apple Pie
Amasake Frosting
Amasake Fruit Drink
Ginger Amasake Drink

Sea Vegetables

One of the most difficult and unusual additions to our diet has been the use of sea vegetables. I often chuckle when I see the expressions on friends' faces when I tell them I eat wakame or kombu.

When I first looked at these black, weird-shaped vegetables I didn't know where to begin. With practice we gradually began adding small amounts of them to our already existing recipes.

For example:

> We added arame to oatmeal and to salads.
> We added nori to popcorn and as lettuce in sandwiches.
> We added hijiki to stir frys and vegetable pancakes.
> We added kombu to our pressure-cooked rice and other grains.

We continually find new ways to add these and have fun in the process.

How to Use Sea Vegetables

1. Wash, and use sea vegetables in cooking grains. Kombu works especially well. Just take one strip of kombu and put it in the bottom of the pressure cooker or pan. Then add rice, millet, or any grain on top of the kombu.

2. Use the soaking water from sea vegetables in soups, dips, sauces, and dressings, or in sautéing vegetables.

3. Use toasted nori on top of vegie burgers, crumbled in salads, on pizza, and in casseroles. Also good crumbled on popcorn or hot cereals.

4. Cooked hijiki and arame can be chopped finely and added to hot cereals, pancakes, grains, salads, casseroles, and muffins.

Basic Cooking Methods for Sea Vegetables

1. Soak sea vegetables in enough cold water to cover for 10 to 15 minutes.

2. Hijiki and arame can be boiled for 3 to 5 minutes, then cooked over low heat for 20 minutes.

3. Arame can be soaked and used without cooking.

4. Wakame and kelp can be rinsed and sauteed or boiled.

5. Kombu and mekombu can be rinsed and boiled.

6. Nori can be toasted in oven at 350°F for about 10 seconds or over a burner and used as a snack or topping for salads and casseroles.

Recipes Using Sea Vegetables:

Arame Oatmeal
Stuffed Nori
Nori Noodles in Broth
Rice Tempeh Rolls
Cucumber Wakame Salad
Sea Noodle Tostada
Sea Vegie Tostada
Oriental Coleslaw
Millet Salad
Hijiki Salad
Hijiki Salad Dressing
Hijiki Noodles
Hijiki and Dried Tofu
Fried Rice

Natural Foods Glossary

Agar-Agar – see kanten.

Amasake – A pudding made from sweet brown rice. Can be used as a creamy base for desserts or thinned as a beverage.

Arame – Thin, black sea vegetable, almost like noodles. Good in salads, soups, sauces, and even in some desserts.

Arrowroot – A starchy flour used as a thickener. Less processed than cornstarch, it lasts indefinitely when stored in a cool, dry place.

Bancha Tea – Tea made from twigs, stems, and leaves of Japanese tea bushes. A pleasant beverage that aids digestion.

Barley-Malt Syrup – A natural sweetener made from sprouted, dried barley.

Brown-Rice Syrup – A thick syrup similar in appearance to honey, made from brown rice. It can be used to replace honey or sugar in desserts and sauces.

Brown-Rice Vinegar – Vinegar made from fermented brown rice. Rice vinegar enhances the flavor of plain rice. Also used in salad dressings, soy-based dips, and sauces and serves as an excellent pickling agent.

Burdock – A long narrow dark-brown root vegetable usually grated or chopped and sautéed or simmered in soup broth.

Carob Powder – A sweet, brown powder with flavor similar to that of chocolate, with less fat and no caffeine. Because carob is sweet, little or no additional sweetener is needed in baked goods.

Daikon – Long, white Japanese radish. Eaten raw, cooked, stir fried, or pickled. Fresh daikon keeps for up to ten days refrigerated.

Dashi – Japanese stock made by simmering a six-inch strip of

As Easy As 1, 2, 3

kombu in a pot of water. Shiitake or soy sauce may also be
added.

Ginger Root – Rootstock of ginger plant, grated or sliced and
used for seasoning. One tablespoon grated, fresh ginger
equals about one-eight teaspoon dried, ground ginger.

Gomashio – A condiment to sprinkle over grains or vegetables, made from roasted sesame seeds ground with sea salt in
a proportion of from 10:1 to 20:1.

Hijiki – Sea vegetable similar to arame but thicker and with a
more robust flavor. Can be used in soups and salads.

Kanten – A gelatin substitute derived from algae. One tablespoon of flakes thickens one cup liquid.

Kombu – Flat sea vegetable, about one inch wide, similar in
shape to lasagne noodles. Great in soups and good to enhance
flavor of cooked rice and beans.

Kuzu (or Kudzu) – White starchy powder made from root of
the kudzu vine. Used for thickening soups, sauces, and pud-
dings.

Mirin – Sweet rice wine. Good in dressings, vegetable dishes,
sauces, and glazes. May be made naturally from sweet brown
rice, rice koji, and water.

Miso – A paste made from fermented soybeans and grains.
Used to flavor soups, sauces, and vegetable dishes. Similar to
beef bouillion or gravy in a meat-centered diet.

Mochi – A dumpling or cake made from sweet brown rice.
When baked, mochi puffs up to twice its size.

Nori – Crisp, black sea vegetable in sheets about six inches
square. Good for rolling around rice and great as a garnish
when toasted and crumbled.

Ramen Noodles – Quick-cooking noodles which are great for a
fast, simple meal. Be careful to check ingredients as some ver-
sions contain refined wheat, additives, and artificial flavors.

Sea Vegetables – Usually sold dry, sea vegetables contain

more minerals than most land vegetables.

Seitan – Also called wheat meat. It is made from wheat gluten and makes a good substitute for meat in many recipes.

Sesame Oil – Expressed from sesame seeds. Excellent for salads and sautéing.

Shiitake Mushrooms – These mushrooms add flavor to soups, stews, sauces, and stir frys. Available dried or fresh.

Shoyu – Naturally-brewed soy sauce.

Soba Noodles – Long narrow noodles made from 100 percent buckwheat or combinations of buckwheat and whole wheat.

Somen Noodles – Thin flat whole-wheat noodles.

Soy Milk – A beverage made from soybeans and water. It has less fat and no cholesterol when compared to milk and can be used like milk.

Sweet Brown Rice – A short-grain rice which is sweeter than regular brown rice. It is very sticky when cooked and can be used in baby cereal, rice balls, and sushi.

Tahini – A Middle-Eastern food. It resembles peanut butter but is made from sesame seeds. It can be used as a spread or in sauces, dressings, and desserts.

Tamari – A naturally-brewed soy sauce containing no wheat.

Tempeh – A fermented soybean product. Commonly used to replace meat.

Tofu – A neutral-tasting, cheese-like product made from soy milk. It picks up the flavor of other foods and can be used in sauces, desserts, stir frys, and as a substitute for meat or cheese in main dishes.

Udon Noodles – Thick, flat wheat noodles.

Umeboshi – Plums that have been pickled in salt. Used as a condiment and in sauces and dressings.

Wakame – Sea vegetable often used in miso soup and salads.

Index

122

Index

123

Index